PATRIOT
ON THE
KENNEBEC

PATRIOT
ON THE
KENNEBEC

*Major Reuben Colburn, Benedict Arnold
and the March to Quebec, 1775*

MARK A. YORK

Charleston • London

THE
History
PRESS

Published by The History Press
Charleston, SC 29403
www.historypress.net

Copyright © 2012 by Mark A. York
All rights reserved

Cover art by Sidney Adamson. Courtesy of the Library of Congress.

First published 2012

Manufactured in the United States

ISBN 978.1.60949.500.8

Library of Congress Cataloging-in-Publication Data
York, Mark A., 1953-
Patriot on the Kennebec : Major Reuben Colburn, Benedict Arnold and the
March to Quebec, 1775 / Mark A. York.
p. cm.
Includes bibliographical references and index.
ISBN 978-1-60949-500-8
1. Colburn, Reuben. 2. United States--History--Revolution, 1775-1783. 3. Canadian
Invasion, 1775-1776. 4. Arnold, Benedict, 1741-1801. 5. Maine--Biography. 6. Coburn
family. I. Title.
E207.C74Y67 2011
973.3092--dc23
[B]
2011049608

This book is dedicated to my mother, Norma Colburn York.

CONTENTS

Acknowledgements

O ne who embarks on a project like this has to be grateful for prior scholarship that made a new effort much easier as a result. Kenneth Roberts is the first to thank, for without his work in the 1930s on *Arundel*, a project like mine would not have been possible. The "March to Quebec" journals that he collected at his expense and published for such a use were at the forefront of this historical effort. So, too, the work of Justin Smith, who years later contributed the 1901 photograph of Colburn House taken on a visit related to his two key books on the subject and who located the files of Reuben Colburn in Washington, from whence I tracked them down again. By having the words, dates and actual receipts as primary sources, speculation could be held to a minimum. This was a critical aspect. While Mr. Roberts meant to portray the true picture with this extensive research, he failed in some cases. His ancestors, the Nasons, were elevated to a far greater status in his narrative at the expense of real heroes whose contributions were documented in the primary texts. In fact, there was no reference to them in the texts at all. Colburn, however, was not one of them, but his pivotal role was greatly reduced and quickly dispensed of in the story. There was no mention of Reuben, his brothers or his company of carpenters once the army departed for Quebec. After that, it was strictly "Steven Nason" and "Cap Huff" who tell the parts of the tale they chose through Roberts's eyes.

The false fallibility of the scouts was equally troubling. Instead of adhering to the exemplary record of Dennis Getchell and Samuel Berry, Roberts chose to superimpose a drunken McConkey character in Berry's place, thus blaming local natural sloth, drunkenness and laziness for an incomplete reconnaissance report and, by and large, the failure of the mission. Roberts insinuates this was a "typical" resident found in this part of Maine. Nathaniel Berry, a younger brother, was one of General Washington's private guards, so the Berrys should not be dismissed so lightly, let alone libeled, but in fiction anything goes, especially about the dead, who can't be libeled. The rest of the failures lay with the bateaux, but Roberts had Colburn explain himself on that matter, as no other chose to until James Kirby Martin in 1997. So Roberts gets credit for that, as he should. I am grateful that he gave my grandfather dialogue and hence a real character in *Arundel* that I'm sure he had in real life.

Roberts "gets" Reuben Colburn, but in his dialogue, he left a clue of his prejudice. "I was prepared to mislike Colburn," he wrote in *Arundel*, "for being responsible for Washington's and Arnold's fondness for bateaux; but I had wronged him."

That was when Roberts realized he had no choice but to enter the evidence of the letters from Washington and Arnold, refuting the notion as exhibit A. Good choice. But it revealed the desire expressed by many to blame Colburn for everything. Roberts quickly moved on to simply attacking the inferior Kennebec bateau as compared to an *Arundel* version. But this was petty, as these two rivers were in no way in the same hydrological realm. The Kennebec River at Pittston was a huge waterway large enough for transports and the launching of one-hundred-foot schooners built on its banks. And besides, Arnold's initial complaint was that Colburn had built them too small, not the other way around. Roberts's selective dismissal of my family as a key element in the whole mission in favor of Arnold, and his fictional relative, is laughable (if not damnable). The dismissal of Central Maine local tradition, though as everywhere often faulty, about the stay in Pittston and Fort Western was another example of "Kennebunkport" prejudice that, when held under the objective lens, fell apart quickly. I'm perplexed why Roberts succumbed to selective amnesia when he discovered facts that didn't fit the story he found and wanted to write. The banquet at Howard's and the primary references to such a meal were completely overlooked in favor of others that chose not to mention it. And this, he offered in his nonfiction collection, *Trending into Maine*, was proof of local embellishment. That was a selective bias. What one left out was as telling as what one included. And so it went for the tale of Aaron Burr and Jacataqua, yet Roberts embraced this story word for word in *Arundel*, while dismissing any basis in reality of the whole thing in *Trending into Maine*,[1] when a large part of the legend appeared to be factually true based on direct attribution. His relative wasn't included;

therefore, it must be a "myth," according to the illustrious Maine sage. This logic does not hold up to Mr. Roberts's own primary sources on scene.

It was unclear just whom this relative of his actually was who marched with Arnold to Quebec. Steven Nason was a composite character built, for the most part, around a trader, Steven Harding, who was not a Nason. Then who was this mysterious Nason who so nobly marched with Arnold and whose exploits encompassed the efforts of the Colburns in history? I'm afraid we don't know. If, as Roberts says in "March to Quebec," all the men from *Arundel* were in Captain Goodrich's division, then we find no Nason listed there.[2] He told us briefly about his ancestor in an *Arundel* family profile in *Trending*. Edward Nason, age nineteen, left for Cambridge, where he signed on with Goodrich and then "followed Arnold to Quebec, where he was captured attacking the city, and held prisoner until release in the spring of 1776," he wrote.[3] That may well be, but there was no mention of him in the journals or in Arnold's letters, as is Colburn.[4] But it isn't up to me to prove whether Edward Nason was there or not.[5] Simply, this lack of evidence of his accomplishments and dismissal of our family's contribution in favor of his was surely a work of fiction, which is not always the case in depicting real events. Perhaps this is what drove Roberts to fiction in the first place.

This was perplexing to one with prominent ancestry in this national event, but I could also point out that the "height of land" where Arnold's army crossed into Quebec now bears the name "Coburn Gore" and not "Nason's Notch."

I say Mr. Roberts was a conservative because of certain statements on the record about taxes and the policies of Franklin Roosevelt that placed the author in the Republican camp at the very least. Roberts seemed less appalled by Mussolini and the fascists during his stay in Italy in the '30s than by FDR's handling of domestic and foreign affairs during those turbulent times. Roberts championed an anti-immigrant stance while at the *Saturday Evening Post* in the 1920s and felt many Democratic senators at the time were more traitorous than Arnold ever was. Indeed, many blamed Congress for Arnold's defection, so there was a basis for this. Roberts blamed Wilson and the "sniveling" Europeans in the League of Nations as the worst examples of failure in U.S. foreign policy ever. Yet Harding, Coolidge and Hoover got off scot-free on every account, as if they had not been running the show at all or had ever been given the chance to show how it was done. Roberts was fearless, nonetheless, in his pursuit of a young Adolph Hitler for an interview, and his suspicions of Hitler's potential danger are duly noted.

Many accused perceived appeasers of the same crimes of shortsightedness today, the inability of some to see the obvious future. Roberts also expressed disdain for the "bums and beggars" of the 1930s, as if a "socialist" Roosevelt administration created them from scratch, implying that asking for a handout was easier than finding work that didn't exist at the time. Of course, Mr. Roberts was fortunate enough to have inherited a house, as were his seafaring ancestors. This came in handy as a safe perch from which to preach to the less fortunate. But prediction was much easier looking back than forward. Roberts was more focused on the past than the present, but a certain bias for both periods was evident.

So was his disdain for critics, in the same mode as Ernest Hemingway, although he never wrote of him by name. He was also disdainful of an uneducated public whose popular literary tastes Mr. Roberts found disturbing, and he vowed never "to know how to write" if such fare was required. Roberts was what we would call now an exclamation-pointer. Even in his nonfiction, Roberts proclaimed his inevitable surprise by showering the text with them. Today's training in literature prefers limited use of that particular punctuation, letting the reader decide what is surprising about the statement, but that was his day and way.

Contrary to prior histories, Kenneth Roberts loved Arnold and seemed to forgive his turncoat tradition completely. He even had a sample of Arnold's hair sent by a relative of the general taken from the time of his death. It was brown, not white, as some alleged from disgrace. Roberts extrapolated that Arnold was at peace and in no way anguished in exile. This seemed farfetched, but one gleaned what one wanted from evidence. Arnold did what he did when he did it; that's the only objective way to see him now. He was a great heroic general who, with the help of his Loyalist (some say the Shippens were "neutralists") wife, turned traitor. No one should doubt his ability at Quebec and Saratoga. This was Roberts's main point, but the point has also been made of the author's sympathy for the Loyalist point of view as portrayed in *Oliver Wiswell*. Indeed, for writing this story in the first place, but it was a side that needed portrayal too.

In my family, English Loyalists were the enemy, and the Colburns expelled them from the country for that choice. They were what they were, too. So, my acknowledgement has evolved into an indictment of sorts of Mr. Roberts and his town, but as writers, we go where the facts lead and ask the tough questions. Roberts told us nothing about his opinion of Harry Truman, but one would doubt it would have been positive. Kenneth Roberts left us in 1957 from his sprawling estate, Rocky Pastures, having won the Pulitzer Prize for his historical chronicles of *Arundel*, well deserved. It must have assured him to have Mr. Eisenhower firmly in power and the country in a kind of naïve bubble. I came from that time in which Kenneth Lewis Roberts's life concluded. I think in 2011, we have seen enough of the "Kennebunkport" take on the world. There seemed to be gaps in the "true picture" from those houses of privilege where the Atlantic laps to the front lawns atop rocky cliffs and the image was good times forever, a long way from the ghosts of the haggard bateaux men of Arnold's army.

As a Colburn descendant, I could not be more proud of my family's role in history. The documentary filmmaker Ken Burns once told me that "any investigation into the past was a labor of love." And so it was. The quality of the story I inherited made it easy to love and fight for still, some 228 years later.

Chapter 1

AMERICAN BEGINNINGS

I t was like finding a priceless gem in the attic. When I searched my roots, I found that a mere twenty miles from my hometown in the village of Pittston, Maine, stood the home of a man who was not only significant locally but also nationally: my great-great-great-grandfather—a local hero and a founding father of the state of Maine—Major Reuben Colburn. The Colburns were early immigrants to America, first arriving in 1635 from London, England. In that year, young Edward Colburn settled in Ipswich, Massachusetts, and later founded the town of Dracut on the Merrimack River. His great-grandsons and their legacy are the guides on this American journey. The home still sits on a hill above the Kennebec River where Reuben and his brothers Oliver and Benjamin erected the oak post and beam frame in 1765. That alone is amazing in this day and age.

This family epic is one of the great American tales of all time. When Colonel Benedict Arnold arrived at the shipyard in the front yard of the house in September 1775, history was in the making, and the Colburns were at the forefront among those making it. The journey on the Arnold trail had begun. It is uniquely America's story.

✠

In late November 1775, three bateaux floated listlessly down the Kennebec River through the wilderness in the province of Maine. The flat-bottomed boats with flared sides held several emaciated Patriots, their clothes in tatters, returning from a Herculean effort to transport the infant, 1,100-man ragtag Continental army under the command of Colonel Benedict Arnold to Canada for an attempted attack on British-held Quebec City.

The army still floundered along the Canadian border. Steeped in mires and starving, its volunteers were reduced to eating boiled shot pouches and dogs. The week before, an entire division had given up and returned to Cambridge, from which they had begun in late September. The bateaux drifted on. Around Pishon's Ferry, the snow turned to rain. Thirty miles later, they beached the bateaux at a flat meadow amid a stand of white oaks. At the crest of a gently sloping hill stood a white, two-story colonial house. The flagpole flew the declaration of liberty.

It was the home of Major Reuben Colburn,[1] a shipbuilder and American Patriot. Colburn departed the bateau and ascended the hill to meet his worried wife, Elizabeth. In this yard, America was born, and the battle to keep it had begun those two long months ago.

✠

In the spring of 1761, a wooden sailing ship rounded Arrowsic Point and entered the mouth of the Kennebec River, in the territory of Maine. Onboard was the family of Jeremiah Colburn and his wife, Sarah Jewell, formerly of the town of Dunstable in north central Massachusetts. The banks of this wide river were dense with tall white pines, and white oaks to the water's edge measured over eighteen feet in diameter; Atlantic salmon and alewives proliferated in the streams of the region in such numbers that it appeared one could walk from shore to shore on their backs and never get wet. It was a land of tremendous bounty.

The Colburns were bound for Gardinerstown, a community thirty miles upriver from the coast, where they had been invited to settle by the Kennebec Company of Dr. Sylvester Gardiner, a prominent Boston physician and businessman who owned a vast tract of land in central Maine. There were few settlers in the area at this time and only two forts left over from the French and Indian War: Western at Cushnoc and Halifax at Ticonic. Shallow water stopped the Colburns six miles short of Fort Western, where the family anchored on the eastern side of the river.

Here, there was a flat shelf of land suitable for homes and tall oaks from which ships could be fashioned. Four brothers (Reuben, Jeremiah, Oliver and Benjamin Colburn) and their four sisters (Sarah, Rachel, Lucy and

Hannah) disembarked the vessel on this shelf of land above a small point where a stream entered the river through the woods. Here, they unloaded their belongings and built a house that is still located nearby.

The Colburns and other early settlers founded a village, and soon young Reuben Colburn, then twenty-one, stepped forward as the unofficial leader on that eastern side of the river. In 1765, Reuben acquired 250 acres from his father, Jeremiah. Ten years later, his holdings had grown to a square mile of land. He began work on a house fit for his growing family's needs. He cut and milled the oak timbers for the frame from his own mill and, with the help of his brothers and his neighbors, the Agrys, erected the skeleton on a foundation of local granite. He married Elizabeth Lewis, a French Huguenot, and they had ten children together, all born in the back room of the home on the hill.

At the river beside the home of his parents, the next endeavor was to build a shipyard. While most of the early settlers on the river built boats, Colburn was the only one who had the operation named for him. The Colburn Shipyard was the center of employment in Pittston for years to come. It was also the center of Revolutionary activities in the far north as resentment of England grew.

Reuben Colburn became a fierce Patriot and lobbied hard for separation from England. In those early days, all the best white pine greater than twenty-four inches in girth that once grew in New England were marked with a crown and ordered to be only available for the construction of British galleons. As a result, the widest board found in Reuben's house is exactly twenty-four inches. Reuben claimed local timber for his own business, and soon tall ships were under construction in the yard below Agry's Point. Colburn's partner, Thomas Agry, had a mill on the point that bears his name and worked steadily to provide lumber to the shipyard. The community prospered, but England continued to interfere, imposing excessive taxes and tariffs on colonists' products. The "liberty" pole in the yard of the Colburn House flew the Liberty flag, revealing the family's politics for all to see. With his wealth and connections, Dr. Gardiner was a Loyalist and on his way to being hated in the Patriot community and ultimately exiled.

Oliver Colburn started a militia in anticipation of the certain trouble to come; he would be the military man in the family, a militia captain, but Reuben would attain the rank of major. It wasn't clear at the time when the conflict would occur. Some cowered, some cheered and some instigated the War for Independence.

Before the American Declaration of Independence on July 4 of that familiar year, 1776, there was 1775, the most important year in our history. The year 1775 was an illustrious and turbulent one in which the united colonies actually went to war with Great Britain, the most powerful empire on the face of the earth. They were outmanned, under armed and described as a "rabble in arms." They were poor farmers and small businessmen banding together against an oppressive power that governed their every move and controlled their resources—and thus their livelihoods—with an iron hand.

On February 9, the British Parliament declared Massachusetts in rebellion, and serious debate began in the colonies. About a third of the colonists wanted independence; a third, the more wealthy Tories, remained loyal to the Crown; and the last third were undeclared. The outcome would be up to the first group. These were the Patriots, and they came from all parts of the colonies to eventually take up arms against Britain.

On March 23, Patrick Henry of Virginia delivered his "Give me liberty or give me death" speech in Williamsburg, Virginia. Lieutenant General Thomas Gage, already the commander in chief of British troops in North America, was also appointed governor of Massachusetts and ordered to enforce King George's law in the colony. But the colonists controlled the countryside, and the British retreated to Boston. A party of nine hundred British regulars ventured out to Concord to secure a munitions depot, but Paul Revere and others left their homes in Boston to warn the Patriots in Lexington and Concord. The next day, the shot heard 'round the world was fired, and the Revolution became a reality.

Without regard to failure, John Hancock, Samuel Adams and George Washington launched into one of the most important endeavors the world had ever known. Theirs was an act of treason from which there would be no return. The first rumblings in mid-winter led to the Battles of Breed's and Bunker Hill in June, followed by Washington taking command of the Continental army at Cambridge in July and the campaigns of Benedict Arnold on Lake Champlain and the disastrous expedition to Quebec, culminating in that battle at year's end.

With the engagement against Britain encroaching on the Colburns' fledgling community, finances and resources vital to the cause were difficult to arrange and, for the most part, beyond their modest means. Colburn recognized this vulnerability and moved quickly to gain help from the colony to reinforce the town and the northern territory from being overrun by the British.

We have exerted ourselves to the utmost of our power in order to obtain such a quantity of powder as is necessary in our present situation, but can obtain none.[2]
Committee of the Provincial Congress of the Massachusetts Bay in New England, assembled at Watertown

They were worried about defense and believed that federal help in the area was imperative. It is still one of the basic foundations of the country, and it started here.

Reuben Colburn, like his great-grandfather Edward, who had hopped a ship to come to America in 1635, was a leader ahead of his time, and he must have known that the role required sacrifice for the greater good. His actions backed this up. Diplomacy got one a long way in most circles, but action was imperative.

The communities of Gardinerstown and Colburntown still contained as many Tories as Patriots, the most prominent being Dr. Gardiner himself. Those who were afraid to be on their own without the support of the Crown knew separation would be difficult and were content to remain with the status quo. There was nothing new about this either. As long as rum was cheap, they held fast to this position and conducted their affairs accordingly. The real founding brothers, the Colburns, knew different. They knew the freedom they sought in the northern wilderness had to be defended were it to last. It took courage.

Meanwhile, an ambitious, militarily skilled former apothecary and trader from Rhode Island set a course that would cross with Reuben Colburn's on the way to his becoming one of America's most capable generals and, ultimately, its most infamous traitor—one Benedict Arnold.

Chapter 2

OLD COLBURNTOWN (PITTSTON)

The town of Pittston was built on the backs of many but under the guidance of a select handful of leaders. "In 1761, four brothers, Reuben, Jeremiah, Oliver and Benjamin Colburn, settled above Agry's Point and formed a settlement then known as Colburntown."[1] The boundary was fluid in 1761. In general, two miles above Agry's Point, including where Randolph is now, is where the Colburns stopped. However, they only lived this far north for one to two years until as early as 1762, when Jeremiah bought the land right above the point across the Pittston line drawn in 1779.[2]

All the settlers arrived at roughly the same time—from 1760 until 1775, the year Arnold came to town. In May 1765, Reuben Colburn received the deed of 250 acres of land just above his father Jeremiah Sr.'s place on Old River Road. He had just married Elizabeth Lewis and desired to start a family. On July 5, 1763, Jeremiah acquired "800 acres on the Eastern River owned by Dr. Sylvester Gardiner and others."[3] Reuben made do with this paltry parcel for ten years until, in 1775, he bought a one- by five-mile strip stretching from his house to the east.

Henry Smith came to the area in 1765 after arriving in America as a boy in 1747. On September 23, 1765, he received a deed for five acres of land in what is now the city of Gardiner. Smith decided that Gardiner was not for him, and in 1772, he bought 102 acres on the eastern side of the river from Dr. Gardiner for which he paid 66 pounds, 12 shillings, 4 pence. His acreage was located just above Reuben Colburn's place, and the two became close friends and business associates for the remainder of their eventful lives. Smith, unlike many of his neighbors, was not a farmer. He was a businessman and innkeeper who built an enterprise that included a ferry service to Gardiner. "Smithtown" was the center of activity for years, and the inn fed the many carpenters employed by Reuben Colburn during the furious weeks preceding the Arnold expedition.

"Hogsheads" of rum were stacked deep at the tavern, and business was always brisk. They held the first town meetings there, and Smith was the first moderator of Old Pittston. Reuben Colburn followed in this job, his first in politics. Henry needed a wife, and he didn't have to look farther than his own new neighborhood in the section of old Pittston called Colburntown, the area above Reuben's place to the site of the village where the town of Randolph is today, where the Colburn family first settled in 1761. The daughters of Jeremiah Sr. remained in the village as their brothers spread to the south on their father's newly acquired eight hundred acres. Henry met and married Sarah Elizabeth Colburn, Reuben's younger sister, in 1767. Together, they created Smithtown and remained there for the rest of their lives. Many of the area's future residents descended from them, including half of this author's family.

Henry and Sarah had nine children. Family ties took on a new meaning in Old Pittston and must be seen in the context of the area and the times. Consanguineous marriage was a Puritan pillar. John Smith later married Abigail Colburn, his first cousin and the daughter of his uncle, Major Colburn. Smith was the first to do so but not the last. Little Abigail was just nine months old when Colonel Arnold and the army stayed at the house. In 1795, she was at last out of the house at the age of twenty. In turn, her younger sister Olive followed suit, wedding John Colburn Sr., the son of Reuben's brother Captain Oliver Colburn, in 1807.

The citizens set about the business of creating a town, and the Colburns were among the original signers of the petition as follows:

To the Honorable Council and House of Representatives of the State of Massachusetts Bay.
The Petition of a Number of the Freeholders and other Inhabitants of the Plantation now called Gardinerstown, in the county of Lincoln, within the State aforesaid, humbly sheweth, "That there is now more than fifty Families settled within the said Plantation called Gardinerstown, who in their present situation Labour under many difficulties, and are desirous of enjoying the Priviledges that will arise to them by being incorporated into a Town [by the name of, erased].

Your Petitioners therefore pray that they may be incorporated into a Town...

[Signed,]

Joseph North, Samuel Berry, Nathaniel Berry, John Door, Beniar Door, Richard Thomas, Sr., Oliver Colburn, Henry Smith, Joseph Burns, Thomas Agry, Benj. Colburn, Samuel Norcross, Philip Norcross, Eleazar Tarbox, Andrew Goodwin, John Deni, Eben Thomas, Henry McCausland, Gideon Gardiner, Samuel Oakman, Dennis Jenkins, Samuel Norcross, Jr., James Stackpole, Andrew McCaslen, William Usher, Reuben Colburn, Herman Raffeus, Nathaniel Cole, Thomas Phillbrook, Joseph Haley, Enoch Moffat.[4]

They delivered the document into the hands of the Honorable John Pitt on January 15, 1779.[5] A fortnight later, after final passage, the town was called Pittston, after Mr. Pitt, and so incorporated. Mr. Pitt was a distinguished gentleman of his time and represented Boston in the state legislature. Afterward, he became a justice in the Court of Common Pleas for Middlesex County and died in Dunstable on November 10, 1815, at age seventy-eight.

Dunstable was also the town the Colburns founded in the 1600s and left to settle in Maine. In order to get the incorporation, the name credit went to Pitt, the man with the power to make it happen; little has changed in the world of politics.

It was a rural frontier with brutal winters and the transportation limitations of horses, wagons and sleighs to get around a vast forested landscape. People were in short supply in those days, and the expediency of marriage of daughters was the norm. They didn't have the luxury of time, leisure and selectivity. They were limited to landowners. What would be the use of marrying outsiders who could not provide a house and other resources necessary to start and support a family? The Colburn daughters married well in the first generation.

Dr. Zacharia Flitner arrived in Boston in 1764 after graduating from medical school at Gotha, Germany, on April 29, 1743. "Tradition says he traveled over parts of Europe before joining the Prussian army, to which he was attached as a surgeon for several years previous to coming to America."[6] Through the acquaintance of a Judge North, he was induced to go to the Kennebec region and did so, buying five acres from Dr. Gardiner on September 20, 1765, on the condition that he would build a house and dwell there for seven years. Thus, Dr. Flitner became the first physician in the region to date. Wasting no time, he married Lucy Colburn, Reuben's sister, on November 5, 1765, at Augusta.[7] Flitner moved his family to Lake Maranacook during the Revolution for reasons not recorded. From there, he served as a surgeon in 1779 as a member of Colonel McCobb's Company of militia in General Lovell's brigade for the duration of the war.

After the war, he moved to the east side of Nehumkeag Pond on a plot of land that bordered the east boundary of Reuben Colburn's land, where he lived for the remainder of his years. In 1799, he sold his land to his son Joseph, and he died in 1804. "Lucy lived to be aged, but died before he did. They were interred in the old churchyard near Major Colburn's where nearly all of Pittston's early settlers were laid to rest."[8]

Hannah Colburn married Josiah French of Winthrop, and they lived in that town and had two sons as of 1790.[9] Of them, little is known and recorded. Her sister Rachel married Thomas Jackson in 1782, who with his five brothers all served in the Continental army with legendary status. They lived in Pittston all their lives in proximity to their relatives. Jackson was the son of Michael Jackson and was born in Newton, Massachusetts, in 1751. Rachel, Reuben's other younger sister, was born on the family farm in Dunstable on August 10, 1754. She came north with the family in 1761. She and Jackson had two sons, Thomas Jackson Jr. and Elijah Jackson Sr., known as the "deacon." The latter married Abigail Cutts, of another prominent family in Pittston, and their children seem to have left no descendants in the record.

Oliver settled south of his brothers' places, where the ancestral homes he built still stand. He married Margaret Burns, and they had eight children: five daughters and three sons. His original parcel of land stretched from the Kennebec River east to the shore of Nehumkeag Pond. He built the homes that my grandfather grew up in on each side of what is now Route 27. The order is not clear, but the period was before 1788, when Oliver mysteriously died at age forty-four, uncharacteristically young for the long-lived Colburns. He was a sea captain and sailed the ships that Reuben built in his shipyard. The outcome could have been anything, from lost at sea to picking up malaria on a trip to the West Indies. The records do not say. His grave is nowhere to be found either, adding to the mystery. It is likely he is buried with Dr. Flitner and Samuel Oakman behind the church at Major Colburn's.[10] There is no way to be sure.

Forever known as "Lieutenant," younger brother Benjamin married his second wife, Joanna Tibbetts, at Hallowell in 1777. They had ten children, all raised on the land in Pittston. Like his brothers, he also served on the town council and as a moderator. His living was made farming and helping with the timber operations of his brother Reuben and Thomas Agry.

Agry came to Pittston from Barnstable, Massachusetts, where his family was among the original settlers. He arrived in 1774, settling below Reuben Colburn on a point of land south of where Nehumkeag Creek enters the Kennebec. The land still bears his name. Here, he erected a lumber mill and built ships, partnering with Reuben Colburn and Samuel Oakman. It was here that the oaks from Reuben's land were milled for the bateaux built for Arnold.

The Oakmans, a family who arrived early to Scarborough, Maine, in the 1650s, bought land from Benjamin Colburn in 1772 and also engaged in shipbuilding beside Colburn and Agry. Samuel Oakman was active in the Revolution and was on the Committee of Safety in 1775 with Colburn and Agry.[11] He became one of the most successful residents on the river, surpassing the Colburns and everyone else with the exception of William Gardiner as of 1781, and served the town for many years.

A bachelor, the doctor's son William Gardiner, also a Loyalist who, after the Boston Tea Party "would drink tea" in support of Britain, was all set to be tarred and feathered by the townsfolk, but his friend and Patriot, Captain Nathaniel Berry, son of Samuel, helped him escape by canoe on Cobbosseecontee Pond and then overland to Topsham, where Gardiner was taken prisoner.[12] Ironically, he was tried at the Pownalborough Court House, where John Adams once plied his craft and which was later home to Major Goodwin. Gardiner was sentenced to jail time in Boston, returning after the war when it was safe.

It can't be over-emphasized that this enclave of entrepreneurs on the east side were all revolutionary in their politics. This is quite a contrast to the Loyalist enclave of Pownalborough downstream, where Reverend Bailey and Major Samuel Goodwin favored the politics of the founder, Dr. Gardiner. Goodwin was exiled to Halifax, Nova Scotia, and later Great Britain for his troubles in spite of his great personal wealth. The Patriots of Pittston, led by Reuben Colburn, weren't fooling around: they meant business. America was an idea whose time had come.

Chapter 3

THE TRADER FROM NORWICH

Benedict Arnold was born in Norwich, Connecticut, on January 14, 1741,[1] the son of a hard-drinking sea trader, Benedict III, and his deeply religious wife, Hannah. The Arnolds, William (1587–1675) and his son Benedict (1615–1678),[2] arrived in America in 1635, the same year as Reuben's great-grandfather, Edward Colburn. They were Puritans fleeing the religious oppression of England under the reign of the Stuarts. One could safely assume that the Colburns and the Arnolds felt roughly the same way on the matter. William and Benedict soon found in Massachusetts much the same atmosphere they had left in Stuart England and followed Roger Williams to Rhode Island in 1636, settling in the Pawtuxet River region, where they bought up large tracts of land.[3] This foresight paid off handsomely, and the Arnold family soon ascended to the ranks of the wealthy in this part of the young colony.

Benedict IV's great-grandfather was elected ten times as governor of Rhode Island.[4] But his grandfather, Benedict II, spent most of the wealth, which is amazing in its own right considering the start he had been given. It was an omen of things to come, and Arnold's father pulled up stakes and moved to Norwich, Connecticut, for a new start in 1730. He became a cooper (barrel maker) and married the daughter of the town's founding family. From here, Benedict III remade himself into a successful trader, sea captain, businessman and community member of great stature. But it was a high cliff from which to fall.

Young Benedict was a thrill-seeker, eager as many youths are, and he sought to impress his peers with his athletic prowess. He received an education beyond the reach of most boys, traveling with his father on trading missions to the West Indies, where he learned his father's lucrative craft and developed adeptness with sailing ships that would serve him well. The country of the 1750s was in turmoil with the French and Indian Wars, and young Benedict longed for the thrill and glory of the battlefield. But the British blockade of the West Indies soon drove his father's business into a tailspin, and the elder Benedict devolved into the town drunk while his wife, Hannah, dove deeper into the verses of the Bible.

Benedict IV left school, which was only private for a fee in those days, for a public education was not even a concept yet. The family fortune soon evaporated, and in 1759, his mother passed away. His father's downward spiral finally ended three years later, when he died from his despair as much as anything, stemming from the loss of three daughters to disease, his alcohol abuse but a symptom. Arnold apprenticed himself to his cousins, the Lathrops, as an apothecary, a trade he learned well. But he left to enlist in the militia once in 1759, and it only gave him a brief taste for what would come later.

Back at the Lathrops' place, Arnold, now without parents, unlike Reuben Colburn, continued in the trade of drugs, for which he sailed from the West Indies to Canada. In 1762, he moved to New Haven and set up shop at roughly the same time that Reuben Colburn landed in Maine and started his shipbuilding business. They were ages twenty-two and twenty-three, respectively.

Arnold's shingle proclaimed:

> *B. Arnold*
> *Druggist*
> *Bookseller & C.*
> *From London*
> *Sibli Totique*

The last line translated to: "For himself and for everybody."[5] Arnold's shop was right across the street from the harbor on Water Street in the home of prestigious Yale College. We don't know what Reuben Colburn's sign said, but estimation is in order:

> *Reuben Colburn & Bros.*
> *Shipbuilding, Lumber & C.*
> *Gardinerstown (Pittston circa 1779)*

There is no official motto that could be determined from reliable sources, but honesty would have been a key element. Later, the sign may have changed to include his partner, Thomas Agry. In subsequent years, many of Colburn's shipbuilding neighbors went out on their own in spite of the proximity to one another's operations, but in the early years it was only Colburn and Agry.

Arnold became the quintessential Yankee trader in New Haven. Unlike Colburn, he had a sullied family reputation to hide from. It was hard to believe that three successful generations could be befallen by one, but in Puritan society, that's all it took. New Haven was just far enough away from Norwich that not everyone had heard of Benedict and his father's misfortune.[6] The Lathrops provided Arnold with £500 of operating capital, and he was on his way. So it is clear, then as now, that family connections were a boon to anyone who had them. But not all do, and sometimes shear determination and effort had to make up for a lack of a prestigious starting place in life. The Colburns made it through a group effort, but the parents' initial purchase of eight hundred acres of land and the sale to his sons by Jeremiah was as good a start as one could hope for in any century.

The businesses of both Colburn and Arnold flourished in the years that surrounded the infamous Stamp Act. But other oppressive parliamentary measures passed in England sought to choke the life out of Americans, and Arnold soon reacted against them with fervor in much the same way that Reuben Colburn did in Maine. They had to become activists if their interests were to survive. In short, they were fighting for their livelihoods, and this was only the mid-1760s. Arnold concentrated on securing goods in port before the Stamp Act went into effect in 1765, so he had no time to participate in the public protests that became common on town squares all over the colonies. Then, many just ignored the taxes as illegal, if only in their minds, and continued with business as usual. Arnold was one of these,[7] as was John Hancock, the associate of Reuben Colburn and a fellow Gardinerstown landowner. If the duty could be avoided, it was, but there were Loyalists who dutifully turned in merchants and traders who had no reverence for British taxes on their goods and products.

These individuals met with forceful opposition that became more frequent, especially in Boston, where Colburn's friend and confidant, the brewer and Patriot activist Samuel Adams, and his Sons of Liberty crucified the Loyalists often with tar and feathers and beatings at the very least. It was not a common occurrence in New Haven, however. Arnold led a similar effort when Peter Boles, a customs officer, turned him in. The drunken, boastful Boles, hanging out in Beecher's Tavern, a New Haven waterfront bar, invited a confrontation that Arnold and his employees gladly dealt him. They hauled him outside, gave him forty lashes and ran him out of town, never to return.[8] Arnold later paid a small fine for this affair, but this did little to discourage him in future efforts.

The opposition to King George III rose to a fevered pitch, and the side that Arnold and Colburn took was clear even this early in the game. The monitoring activities of Adams and the Sons led to a repeal of the Stamp Act in 1766, but it was clear this was only the beginning of British oppression. The vigilante approach had to be replaced with a more civil body if the movement were to gain credibility, and this evolved into local Committees of Correspondence, Committees of Inspection and Committees of Safety.[9] The first came in October 1774 in Massachusetts. In 1775, this group authorized the occupation at Bunker Hill. Local chapters formed in all communities, and in Gardinerstown, Reuben Colburn chaired the Committee of Safety at this time.

April the 29th, 1775
Received of Mr. Ruben Colburn the Sum of 12 ponds legal tenner on the
account of Mr. North and others which was subscribed for, to by powder.
Signed, Saml Oakman
The above Reuben Colburn and Saml Oakman were of the Committee of
Safety for Pittston for that year. The committee was composed of:
Wm Gardner
Reuben Colburn
Henry Smith
Saml Oakman
F.W. Flitner[10]

At the same time, to the north came a severe problem for the sea traders of the colonies in the form of the Quebec Act, a "British statute passed in 1774 that greatly expanded the British colony of and instituted French civil law within it. The act was meant to address the conflicting desires of Québec's French-and-English-speaking populations, but it failed as a compromise and led to frustration in the colony." So when Guy Carleton arrived in Québec as lieutenant governor in 1766, he was charged with the task of finding an arrangement that would please the British newcomers and win the loyalty of the French Canadians. This was no easy task, because the French Canadians wanted to keep their civil laws and "worried that the British merchants wielded too much influence." British and colonial traders and merchants such as Arnold also worried because the French Canadians tended to keep all businesses in the family, restricting free trade and available partnerships. Also, an "overwhelming majority of the French Canadians were Roman Catholic, and those of this faith were prohibited from holding political office in Britain and its colonies."[11] Many Protestants of all denominations shared one belief in common: fear of Papists. The path had been set for a struggle that included what some later dubbed the "Fourteenth Colony."

In Gardinerstown, they prepared for conflict, while in New Haven Arnold grew restless. In February 1775, King George declared the colony of Massachusetts Bay to be "in rebellion." He ordered General Gage to serve notice and blockaded Boston Harbor. In New Haven, Arnold had been commander of the militia since 1774 and desired to march off to battle, but the town fathers did not approve this action. Arnold scoffed at their timidity. "Only 'Almighty God' could prevent him," he said. All warriors felt God was on their side, but the Patriots were more justified than most in feeling this way about their cause, as surely no just God could support tyranny. Captain Arnold and his foot guards marched and arrived in Cambridge on April 29.

The local Committee of Safety in Massachusetts, headed by Dr. Joseph Warren, was impressed by Arnold's air of confidence and gumption and elected him and his band of "rabble" to conduct a mission to capture British-held Fort Ticonderoga. Arnold was promoted to the rank of colonel in their militia service. They left in May.

The mission was to capture the cannons so needed back in Boston. But Ticonderoga was in the home turf of Ethan Allen and his Green Mountain Boys from Vermont. The personalities of the two commanders clashed, but they agreed to have Arnold take a "guest-starring" role at the head of the force, if in name only, by virtue of his colonel's commission. The brash boldness that served Arnold well in securing opportunities in his life tended to not win him many friends among his competitors. For Benedict Arnold, this would become an Achilles' heel of sorts. Renegades rarely made it when diplomacy was a necessary component for success. With the leadership squabbling behind them, Arnold, Allen and their men crept to the undermanned British fort at 4:00 a.m. on May 10, 1775, and surprised the lone sentry. The bellicose Allen proclaimed "God's will" was at work by way of his hand, while Arnold stood firmly by his side. They raced upstairs and captured the commander, William Delaplace, with his pants down. It had taken them fifteen minutes, and the artillery was in American hands.

The competition for command at Ticonderoga was a tortured affair that lasted the summer. Eventually, Allen and his boys moved on to their homes but continued to assault the north on their own orders from the provincial congress aside from Arnold's from Watertown, Massachusetts, and the Committee of Safety. Arnold's water assault on Canada from Lake Champlain fell short, upstaged by a simultaneous assault by Allen from the Vermont side, and a rebuffed Benedict Arnold returned to Watertown in August to answer to the committee. It was during this return visit that Arnold first met with George Washington at Cambridge, looking for a new commission with more potential for fame. At the same time, the American shipbuilder Reuben Colburn arrived in Cambridge, looking to help in any way he could. Their paths in history were about to converge.

Chapter 4

BROTHERS IN ARMS

The Colburns of New England

What do we mean by Revolution? The war? That was no part of the revolution. That was only the consequence of it. The revolution was in the minds of the people.[1]
—*John Adams*

In August 1775, on a muddy trail through the pine and hardwood forests of the lower Kennebec River on the New England coast, an American Patriot, Reuben Colburn, made his way to Cambridge on horseback, hoping to get involved in the oncoming war against Britain. He was thirty-five and wore a three-cornered hat, characteristic of the time, knee britches, a long coat and black boots to the knee. At his side hung a long sword in a scabbard inscribed with the initials "R.C." He had been summoned by General George Washington to serve on a secret mission.

In Colburntown, Reuben's brothers were at work in the shipyard and mills and had started a militia to protect the young community, as was the policy in all the colonies at the time. "Captain" Oliver Colburn was widely known as the commander of the Colburn Militia, this local group of minutemen. Younger brother Benjamin was a lieutenant, and Reuben became known as the major, although evidence exists suggesting that in 1775, during the expedition with Arnold, he was still a captain. Receipts on record and published by Justin Smith reveal that Samuel Berry, one of the scouts, called him "Capt. Reuben Colburn."[2] Family legend always has held that it was Oliver who followed Arnold upriver, and Reuben stayed at home to supervise the operation. Now it is apparent that only Reuben went with Arnold on the fateful trip, and Reuben was the leader of the company of artificers.[3]

This is further evidence of the unreliability of oral history in determining the true course of human events, what Kenneth Roberts called "the gingerbread demon Local Tradition."[4] No one needed to write Oliver a receipt for anything, as he just worked for his brother, as did younger brother Benjamin. Reuben was always the brain of the operation, and he kept accurate business records, so the receipts were all written to him, not Oliver.

While Reuben Colburn labored at his shipyard and organized the new community, Benedict Arnold was busy building a military career to escape from his successful, if mundane, business as a sailing merchant and druggist. He longed for action and the glow of the spotlight. Most of all, he longed for recognition and the power that is the result. Both men just had to be involved in the effort to launch America; they couldn't stay out of the fray. The two men had never met. Both were major players and on paths that were bound to cross. Neither knew it until all the pieces of the puzzle fell into place. Their two paths grew closer and finally crossed in August 1775.

Colburn would make three trips in that fateful summer. The colonists, beleaguered by tariffs, taxation and the heavy-handedness of King George III, finally had enough. In April of that year, the Continental Congress picked George Washington as the commander of the Continental army, and he set out for Cambridge, where he could prepare to confront the British redcoats. The ragtag army encamped there while the British ships formed a blockade of Boston Harbor.

Colonel Benedict Arnold, fresh from a victory at Ticonderoga with Ethan Allen and the Green Mountain Boys, made his way to Watertown, Massachusetts, where he plotted to get a real command from Washington. In early August, at an Abenaki camp in a clearing in the forest where the Androscoggin and Sheepscot Rivers joined the Kennebec at a place called Merrymeeting, Reuben Colburn arrived in a procession of canoes from his home in Colburntown, where he had entertained the Indian chiefs of the tribes of St. Francis the previous night. With him was Swashan, the great chief. At the camp, Colburn met Paul Higgins, a colonist and friend who lived with the Abenaki by choice and who had organized a similar convention of his own and led them all south, overland on the final leg to Cambridge, hopeful to enlist the Abenaki in the American cause.[5]

As with Arnold, Colburn also had never met the legendary Virginian, Washington, but Colburn's shipyard and lumber mills were widely known throughout the territory. Still, it is not known if Washington had ever heard of him before. Yet Colburn marched into the Continental army camp in early August with "Chief Swashan and four other Indians, decked out with massive earrings and wampum collars,"[6] in tow and gained an audience with His Excellency, General Washington.

Colburn found Cambridge a squalid encampment of tents, makeshift mud huts, horses and assorted livestock. There were no uniforms and little food when Washington arrived that April to take his command. He'd worked diligently to improve the conditions, but things were far from ideal or even functional. Washington implemented strict rules governing the conduct of the unruly amateur forces in hopes of making a real army out of them, but thus far it was a haphazardly, and in some cases reluctant, rebel force. The recruits needed money and worried for their families back home all over the colonies. From Washington, they sought solutions, and from them, he expected service.

The southern patrician Washington quickly took a disliking to the rabble-like New Englanders, whose belief in bottom-up democracy supplanted his belief in southern aristocracy. "There is an unaccountable stupidity in the lower class of these people," he wrote to Philip Schuyler.[7]

Headquarters for Washington was the former Vassall House at 105 Brattle Street, built in the Georgian style for John Vassall, a wealthy Loyalist, and his family. Vassall had abandoned his mansion for Boston in September 1774 when the Revolution finally broke out.[8] It was a stately building with four pillars framing the main entrance and two great chimneys on the roof.

Troops stationed from Roxbury to Charlestown came to receive him when he arrived on July 2, 1775,[9] and the sailcloth tents occupied by the Marblehead Mariners regiment still surrounded the great house when Colburn, Higgins and his Abenaki procession arrived on July 14. They strode up the long, gentle slope dotted with elms, past the encamped troops. At the door, Colburn addressed the guard, who announced their arrival to Washington while the scraggly soldiers looked on. The guard led them into Washington's office, which was to the right of the main entrance in the dining room. It was the room where he entertained guests, planned the response to the siege and, after this visit, planned the attack on Quebec.

No recorded transcript of this meeting exists, but Washington reported the positive results the very next day. Colburn introduced himself and then presented the chiefs for enlistment as Washington stood behind his desk opposite the fireplace. Swashan made his own speech pledging allegiance to the colonies.

The surprised Washington, thought by later historians[10] not to have much use for Indians (a position that is largely unfounded), listened intently. Swashan promised many of his people would fight for the American cause in the northern wilderness they knew intimately and which was the potential target for an American invasion. Washington's reply to Philip Schuyler, in fact, reveals his pleasure with the Indians and with Reuben Colburn. "Yesterday Sen-night arrived at the camp in Cambridge, Swashan, the Chief, with four other Indians of the St. François tribe, conducted thither by Mr. Reuben Colburn, who has been honorably recompensed for his trouble," Washington wrote. "The above Indians came hither to offer their service in the cause of American liberty, have been kindly received, and are now entered the service. Swashan says he will bring one half of his tribe and has engaged 4 or 5 other tribes if they should be wanted. He says the Indians of Canada in general, and also the French, are greatly in our favor, and determined not to act against us."[11]

Colburn was paid thirty-five pounds, sixteen shillings for transporting the Indians to Watertown from Kennebec River on August 17, 1775,[12] so Washington was accurate in his testimony to Schuyler on the matter. He was pleased.

The aftermath of the Battles of Lexington and Concord meant there would be no return. With the first shot fired, the physical actions of the war had begun, and for Reuben Colburn and other notable Patriots, it hadn't come too soon. John Hancock had been named president of the first Continental Congress. Hancock was a business associate and good friend of Reuben Colburn. Colburn would later house and provide guidance to a wayward nephew of Hancock's. John Hancock was a frequent guest at Colburn's house in Colburntown before and after his terms as governor of Massachusetts following the war, when he visited his timber holdings in the area. There isn't any evidence that, despite his powerful position in the new nation, he influenced Washington to use the services of Reuben Colburn in the expedition to Quebec. Colburn appears to have engineered the opportunity of his own accord. Leaders, by nature, tend to attract one another.

Washington knew he needed all the help he could muster and was impressed enough with the gumption of Colburn to keep him and his enterprise in mind for the imminent invasion of Canada. In fact, Colburn's forward-thinking act might just have convinced Washington to go ahead with the plan. Meanwhile, on the western front in Watertown, Arnold was doing his best to get a command from Washington. Like Colburn, Arnold was driven—perhaps on a different level, but driven nonetheless. They believed in the concept of America when many did not.

Mister, I believe in Washington and Arnold.
—*Reuben Colburn, from* Arundel

The expedition was on Washington's mind in this note to Philip Schuyler on August 20:

The Design of this Express is to communicate to you a Plan of an Expedition, which has engaged my Thoughts for several Days. It is to penetrate into Canada by Way of Kennebeck River, and so to Quebeck by a Rout ninety miles below Montreal…if you are resolved to proceed, which I gather from your last Letter is your Intention, it would make a Diversion that would distract Carlton, and facilitate your Views. He must either break up, and follow this Party to Quebeck.[13]

The intersection was inevitable, and it came on August 21, 1775. Arnold received his command of 1,100 men from General Washington, and Colburn's name was passed on with it. Washington had summoned Colburn back to Cambridge to attend to specifics recorded in Colburn's receipt of August 20.[14] Colburn wrote Washington a short note acknowledging the receipt of a down payment on his expenses:

Cambridge, Aug. 20th 1775,
Then received from Genl. Washington the sum of ten pounds lawful money, for the purpose of building Batteaux for the use of the Continental Army.
Signed,
Reuben Colburn[15]

It was written on the second of the three trips Colburn made to Cambridge that month in preparation for the expedition. While there, Arnold wrote him a letter from Watertown requesting that he build two hundred bateaux with paddles and setting poles. The time to fill the order was short.

Mr. Reuben Colburn, Sir:
His excellency, General Washington, desires to inform yourself how soon, there can be procured, or built, at Kennebec, two hundred light Battoes capable of carrying six or seven men each, with their provisions & baggage, say 100 lbs to each man, the boats to be furnished with four oars, two paddles, and two sitting poles each, the expense of building them & wheather a sufficient quantity of nails can be procured with you. You will

also inquire, what quantity of fresh beef can be procured at Kennebec, and the price—at Newbury you will inquire the size and strength of the two armed vessels wheather bound on a cruise or not.

Also the condition the armed vessels are in at Kennebec, you will also get particular information from those people who have been at Quebec, of the difficulty attending an expedition that way, in particular the number & length of the carrying places, wheather low, dry land hills or swamp. Also the depth of water in the river at this season, wheather an easy stream or rapid—also every other intelligence which you judge may be necessary to know, all of which you commit to writing. Dispatch an express to his Excellency as soon as possible, who will pay the charge expense you may be at in the matter.

I am sir, your humble Svt.
Benedict Arnold[16]

In essence, Colburn was instructed to do everything and have it done by the time Arnold arrived. It was a tall order. Colburn sped on horseback back to Colburntown and set his men to work. He had little time and even less dried lumber. Now committed, Reuben vowed to prevail in the service of his country despite these handicaps. With the operation underway, once again he returned to Cambridge, probably arriving on September 2.

Washington forged ahead, arranging a fleet of ships to transport the army to Maine. "You are hereby authorized and empowered," wrote Washington to Nathaniel Tracy on September 2, "to take up for the service for the said colonies, as many vefsels as shall be necefsary for the transporting a body of troops to be detached from this army on a secret expedition."[17] These vessels were to depart from Newburyport, northeast of Boston, to the Kennebec River. There were eleven transports in all.

Washington's letter, delivered to Colburn on September 3, 1775, confirmed the arrangement:

Mr. Rheuben Colburn, of Gardinerstown upon the Kennebec in the province of Massachusetts Bay.

You are to go with all expeditions to Gardinerstown upon the Kennebec and without delay proceed to the constructing of 200 Batteaux to run with 4 oars each; 2 paddles & 2 setting poles to be also provided to each Batteaux. You are to engage a company of men, consisting of artifices, carpenters, and guides to go under your command to assist in such services as you and they may be called upon to execute. You are to purchase 500 bushells of Indian corn to provide the workmen employed in the building the Batteaux.

You are also to bespeak for all the pork & flour you can from the inhabitants upon the river Kennebec, & a commissary will be immediately sent from the Commissary General to agree and pay for the same, you will also acquaint the inhabitants; the commissary will have orders to purchase Sixty barrels of salted beef of 220 Lbs. each barrel.

You are to receive Forty Schillings Lawful money for each Batteaux, with the oars, paddles and setting poles included; out of which you are to pay artifices, & for all the provisions, Nails, etc., they shall expend.

Given this day at Head Quarters at Cambridge this 3rd day of Sept. 1775.

G. Washington[18]

There was precious little time, but Arnold's earlier letter got Reuben going on the intelligence division of the operation. He hired Dennis Getchell of Vassalborough to scout the river for obstacles both human and geological. Colburn himself had never been that far up the river that lay at his door. Getchell and Samuel Berry, the best mountain man in Gardinerstown, set out for the Dead River in early September in the company of Natanis, an Abenaki Indian who had a camp in that area and was a cousin of Colburn's Abenaki friend Sabatis. Getchell and Berry refer to Natanis as "our Indian pilot." On September 13, a messenger arrived at Colburn's shipyard with a letter:

Vassalborough, Sept. 13, 1775,

Sir, In compliance with your orders I proceeded with Mr. Berry on our intended journey to Quebec as follows—Friday Sept. 1, we set out and got on Saturday to Garrards at Skowhegan falls, 24 miles distance. Rainy weather. Sunday 3rd, we arrived at Norridgewock 12 miles distance. Rainy weather, Monday 4th. We arrived at Carrytunk falls. 18 miles distance, swift water & shoal. Tuesday 5th, we reached the great carrying place, water & shoal & swift, distance 18 miles. Wednesday 6th, we got to Windy Pond in the great carrying place, distance ? Miles. Thursday 7th, we arrived at an Indian camp 30 miles up Dead River, good water.

Here we got intelligence from Indians that was stationed here by Gov. Charleton as a spy to watch the motions of an army of officers that was daily expected from New England. That there were spies on the head of the Chaudière River & down the river some distance there was stationed a regular officer & six privates; they positively declared that if we proceeded any farther, he would give information & official possessions of our designs, as otherwise he should betray the trust reposed in him—but not withstanding his threats, we thought it of the moment to get all possible intelligence & went the 8th 30 miles up the river in fast water.

But, finding the water greatly threat, and mating with something new, we returned to the camp—when we arrived "our Indian pilot"[19] thought it dangerous to proceed any further, declined going with us. In the time of our absence he confired with an Indian squaw of whom he got intelligence, that all the young Indians for that quarter had gone to Johnson, but the 2nd LT a commission from Charleton, that at Sartigan the settlement on the Chaudière River, there was a great number of Mohawks that would have destroyed us if we had proceeded & that the spy hourly expected the arrival of three canoes of Indians.

We found the carrying places greatly passable. The water in general, great on arrival the last dry season. The trees are smashed as far as we went and the way is as direct as may be found.

Thus far sir, agreeable to your orders, and the segment of our power have we decided on our intended tour with esteem sir.

Your humble Servts Dennis Getchell, Samuel Berry.

Sir, The above is a copy of a letter I drafted for the above gentlemen and at the request of Mr. Getchell I now send it to you Mr. Reuben Colburn.

I am, yours, Remington Hobby.[20]

Hobby was the town moderator of Vassalborough, employed for his writing skills for this task. Natanis provided key information and prevented Getchell and Berry from stumbling into enemy hands. Had that happened, the above letter would not have come, and Colburn would have had nothing to report to Arnold when he arrived. Colburn's role in providing the intelligence in advance of the army is evidence of the high level of trust placed in him by Washington. Colburn's scouts more than held their own in assessing the situation that lay ahead of them. Colburn's close relationship with Sabatis and Natanis—the two brothers, figuratively speaking, key players who were to figure highly in the intrigue to come—was important. Colburn's influence knew no bounds in the territory of Maine.

But why use bateaux? Washington and Arnold decided on bateaux long before they found Colburn to build them, as Washington's orders indicate. The Kennebec version of the craft was flat-bottomed and rode low in the water. They were never meant to scale rapids and waterfalls.

Locally, river drivers tended to log rafts from them, and they worked fine for that purpose. I have tested well-built modern replicas and wouldn't want to carry them very far either. The fact that in August in a shipbuilding region all available dried lumber was already in use is a pivotal point. There is no evidence of stores of dried lumber and no time to transport it to Colburntown if there had been. Some responsibility lies with the "mustermaster back in Cambridge" for accepting the "eager plowboy as an experienced bateauman."[21] Arnold, by Washington's orders, specifically asked for recruits experienced with bateaux and who were "active woodsmen."[22] In most cases, he got neither. Many of the bateaux, which had to be built slapdash due to time constraints and materials, did leak and were badly built, that much is true. Nevertheless, the community was engulfed by the event, and its patriotic enthusiasm for the revolutionary effort was unbounded.

Hanson wrote:

> *Arnold's expedition to Quebec concerned the settlers of Gardinerstown in a particular way, inasmuch as Major Colburn had been commissioned by General Washington to build two hundred bateaux in his shipyard for use by Arnold's army. The major lived in what is now Pittston, about two miles below Gardiner in a house, which is still standing. He built the bateaux of pine, ribbed with oak. But the pine was green and the bateaux were cursedly heavy to tote, each carrying six or seven men, propelled by four paddles and two poles.*[23]

Colburn and his partner, Thomas Agry, who operated the mill on the point at the mouth of Nehumkeag Stream, must have been immediately concerned. They did what they had to do under the circumstances: cut green pine planks and tar the hell out of the butted seams. This worked well in shaping wet wood when allowed enough time to dry in place on the frame. There was no time for this. It has been alleged that the bateaux should have been left in the water to swell.[24] They were furiously nailed together and left to dry on the bank of the river, as the shoreline had to be left open for the landing parties departing the transports with men and supplies when Arnold and the army finally arrived.

Canoes had their own problems, as guide Nehemiah Getchell later found out on the Dead River.

Kenneth Roberts's dialogue for Reuben Colburn is true to character as I see it, although inferential: "They want bateaux and I give them canoes!

Then what happens when things go wrong? God ain't to blame! The weather ain't to blame! Reuben Colburn's to blame! Will I get my money for them? God knows! I won't if we don't whip England!" Colburn's mission was to see that they did.

But the main factors—such as lack of seasoned wood at that time of the year and the short, last-minute time frame—governed Colburn's choices. Then there was the matter of nails or the near-certain lack thereof. Given the slow, time-consuming process of forging the individual hobnails of the period, there couldn't have been enough to go around, so the workers did what they had to do: short nail the side rails to the frames.[25]

Colburn had been operating at a feverish pace arranging all this while the crew constructed the bateaux. The question of using bateaux was the idea of Washington and most likely Arnold himself, due to his experience with such craft, although they seemed not to know exactly what that meant in technical terms. They probably had a larger version in mind, such as was used on Lake Champlain. Colburn built what was used locally, unaware of the type of transport General Washington wanted. Furthermore, most of the construction took place as Colburn traveled back and forth to Cambridge, seeing to the financial and political details of the operation—not an excuse in any way, but no less a fact.

This miscommunication is responsible for any design flaws. Colburn was compelled to employ locals who weren't experienced in ship-craft because of the large, hasty order, further contributing to the construction problems. "But it does not follow that the boat-builders were really to be blamed," Justin Smith wrote.[26] These particular bateaux were to be thrown away anyway, and "the need for strong boats could not have been understood at Cambridge, and perhaps it was not at Colburn's."[27] He simply did what he was asked to do, regardless of the degree of difficulty. "Certainly there was no sign of a guilty conscience on Colburn's part, for he marched with the army close within Arnold's reach."[28]

Nearly all of the 1,100 men departed from Colburn's yard, with many lingering for three days. The shipyard was a flurry of activity in the weeks preceding the arrival of Arnold on September 22, 1775. Colburn had to arrange for maps of the territory from surveyor Samuel Goodwin of Pownalborough, whose Tory leanings did little to discourage Colburn. "While at Gardinerstown, Arnold received the report of the scouts, Getchell and Berry, whom Washington had ordered Colburn to send to reconnoiter the route (they had gone as far as the Dead River), and he picked up some rough maps that had been prepared by Samuel Goodwin."[29] This is further proof that the intelligence planning and the resulting meetings of the commanders and Arnold for the mission were held at Colburn's. Fort Western was nothing more than a pit stop. The hub of the whole operation was Colburn's, in planning, bateaux building and stockpiling of foodstuffs, as well as the initial military encampment.[30]

Goodwin's reply, written as the expedition was in progress:

Pownalborough, (Maine).
October 17, 1775
To His Excellency George, Washington, Esq.
Sir:
According to your Excellency's verbal orders, by Colonel Benedict Arnold, I supplied him with a plan of the sea-coast, from Cape Elizabeth to Penobscot, and the River Kennebeck to the several heads thereof, and the several carrying places to Ammeguntick Pond [Lake Megantic] *and Chaudière River (which Ammeguntick empties into said Chaudière River, which Chaudière empties into the River St. Lawrence, about four miles above Quebeck); and the passes and carrying places to Quebeck; and also made several small plans for each department, for their guide; and also gave him a copy of a journal which represented all the quick water and carrying places to and from Quebeck, both ways, viz., east and west; the west is the way to go, and the east to come. I think it would be for the general interest for you to have a copy of said plan, etc., and then you would be a judge of what would be best to be done...I will copy one for you, and wait on you with it, and give you the best intelligence I can, as I think I know as much of this country as any one, as I have been travelling, surveying, and settling this part, ever since the year 1750...*
Samuel Goodwin
N.B. Mr. Reuben Colburn informed me you wanted a plan. I thus began it about 3 weeks before Col. Arnold arrived.[31]

Major Goodwin wanted Washington to approve the concept of laying out a road to Quebec Province, from which he would benefit as a speculator in Maine lands.[32] Colburn was to stay behind and see to the continued construction and then follow the army north with his company of artificers (carpenters). But Arnold came into possession of the map and journal of Colonel John Montresor long before he arrived in Gardinerstown, so the charge of misleading maps provided by Colburn via the Tory Goodwin are unfounded.[33] The distance of the route was thought to be 180 miles but turned out to be closer to 350.[34] The distance discrepancy of the route—what there was of it—was the order of the day and not the result of deliberate conspiracy.

In 1761, Montresor, an engineer for the British army, explored the unknown region between Quebec and the Kennebec River (Maine). His account of this journey later fell into the hands of Benedict Arnold,[35] who used it as a guide for his expedition against Quebec in 1775.[36]

It seems as if I have fight this whole damn war by myself.
—*Reuben Colburn, from* Arundel

The crew had to be paid in corn and hope, not to mention rum.

These people up here will do without most anything, if their money's low, but they've gotta have rum.
—*Reuben Colburn, from* Arundel

In all, Colburn received £26 from Washington and Arnold. Records indicate he spent over £500 on the operation. In those days, that represented a considerable sum, worth more than his house and barn, according to tax records. The money was supposed to be a down payment against the final bill to be approved by the Continental Congress. Even with his friend John Hancock[37] at the helm, the money never materialized. It was worse for the townspeople of Colburntown, who weren't as well off as Colburn. He paid them out of his own pocket after the money from Washington was long spent, and he held fast to the hope of promised funds, and his country's need, to sustain him in seeing the operation to fruition.

What Colburn didn't know at the time was the practice of supplying the new army by expropriation. "From the beginning of the war, the Continental Army in emergencies seized whatever it needed. Such action gave rise to many claims for compensation."[38] Colburn at least had a legitimate contract for his services. Nevertheless, with suspicions of nonpayment in mind, during that hectic month he went from citizen to citizen and procured the necessary barrels of salted beef, pork, fish, corn and flour, just as Washington had ordered. He assembled all of it in the yard alongside the bateaux assembly line at the river's edge. The operation was an economic boon for the area.

Carpenters all up and down the river came to Colburn's shipyard to work on the bateaux. Colburn selected the best to travel with him to Quebec. It was probably the best detail on the mission, but little did they know at the time just how bad things would get.

In Cambridge, Arnold assembled 1,100 men. Some volunteered, and some were chosen by lottery. Mostly, the soldiers just wanted to get out of the depressing squalor of Cambridge. This is why the screening question of boatmanship accumulated so many instant experts. The regiments consisted of ten companies of musket men and three of riflemen from Pennsylvania and Virginia, the latter led by the illustrious Captain Daniel Morgan of Winchester, Virginia, already legendary for his service in the French and Indian War. Fitting with his frontiersman status (he was a cousin of Daniel Boone), Morgan dressed in buckskins, unlike most military types of the day. His unconventional approach would come in handy on this mission. The Pennsylvania companies included two "soldiers' wives."[39]

The recruits milled about while Arnold and the quartermaster accumulated the equipment and addressed pay issues. They all wanted a month's pay in advance. This would be the last pay they would see for a long time, and for many this was the last time. Finally, on September 11, Arnold reviewed his troops on the Cambridge parade grounds. They would have to do. The rifle companies left first, moving north that evening, and they reached the mouth of the Merrimac River below Newburyport by September 13.

A battalion under the command of Lieutenant Colonel Christopher Greene and Major Timothy Bigelow, including the medical detail of Dr. Isaac Senter and staff, caught up with Morgan and the riflemen on September 15 in Newburyport, where the transport ships awaited. The remaining five companies commanded by Lieutenant Colonel Roger Enos and Major Return J. Meigs left on September 13 and arrived on September 16. Arnold had a four-man staff and a chaplain. By Washington's prior arrangement with Newburyport merchantman Nathaniel Tracy, the transports awaited the army. Glorious vessels they were not, described as a squalid collection of "dirty Coasters and fish boats." Like most Revolutionary War domestic financiers, Tracy never received the promised compensation.

In these craft, Arnold's army set sail for Kennebec. In fair winds, they soon rounded the point at Popham and proceeded upstream past Georgetown. After one sloop became lost in the labyrinth of Merrymeeting Bay, where the two great rivers Androscoggin and Kennebec meet, requiring a rescue mission delay, Arnold's sloop, *Broad Bay*, docked at Pownalborough Courthouse, where he obtained the arranged maps from Goodwin before pushing on to Colburn's shipyard.

Hanson wrote:

It was an exciting day when Arnold and his army—1,100 men in all— arrived in Gardinerstown. A mixture of "adventurers, would-be soldiers, patriots, and hangers-on," they had walked from Cambridge to Newburyport, and boarded the eleven schooners there available at Gardinerstown, with equipment including 500 bushels of corn and 60 barrels of salt pork, they boarded the bateaux and continued on that ill-fated journey.[40]

There is no doubt as to the location of the start of the expedition once on scene in Maine. The Reverend Jacob Bailey, the Loyalist pastor of Pownalborough, wrote, "200 bateaux were built at Colburn's." The trip started at Colburn's shipyard in Colburntown. This is where all ships had to stop at that time of the year because of the depth of the water and the sandbars present between Colburn's and Fort Western.

"The lessening depth of water in the Kennebec," Smith wrote, "made it impossible to go all the way to Fort Western, about nine miles above Colburn's; and in fact some went but a little distance, if any above the shipyard."[41]

With the arrival of the transports above Agry's Point, Captain Simeon Thayer and the other journalists report disembarking at Colburn's:[42] "Sept. 22. Went on shore with Col. Arnold at Capt. Copelins [Colburn], where there were one hundred men to row the bateaux to Fort Western."[43]

Surveyor John Pierce saw it this way: "Friday Sept. 22. Cast anchor about 11 O'clock in a place in the river called Gardner Town where was a liberty pole erected and 2 saw mills and a number of good dwelling houses on the right of the river-battoes all lying on shoar ready to receive our detachment, about 60 houses in said town."[44]

Private Abner Stocking also confirms the need to stop at Colburn's shipyard: "Sept. 20. By the evening we floated to within 6 miles of Fort Western, where we were obliged to leave our sloops and take to our bateaus."[45]

John Joseph Henry, a judge in later years, said this in his account: "We ascended the river to Colburn's shipyard; here we left our vessels and obtained bateaux, with which we proceeded to Fort Western."[46]

Dr. Isaac Senter had this to say:

Friday Sept. 22nd. Passed Pownalborough ere we arrived at Gardner's Town, where a number of battoes were preparing for our reception after the transports became useless. These were not quite finished. Sept. 23rd.

Arrived at Fort Western at 10 o'clock in the morning. We were now come to a rapid in the river, beyond which our transports could not pass. Most of them were left at Gardner's Town, where the bateaux were built, and the troops disembarked from them into bateaux, except those who were obliged to take land carriage. The bateaux were made of green pine boards, which made them somewhat heavy.[47]

Captain Eleazer Oswald, writing for Arnold:[48] "Thursday. 21—Proceeded as far as Gardinerstown. Friday 22—This morning arrived three of the transports; were employed the whole day in forwarding the men, provisions, bateaus, &c., to Fort Western; engaged two caulkers, some guides, and assistants."[49]

Major Return Jonathan Meigs is the only journalist who mentions the short amount of time allotted Reuben Colburn to build the bateaux and round up the provisions. He includes it in his entry for September 20:

I would mention here that this day makes fourteen only, since the orders were first given for building 200 battoes, collecting provisions for levying 1,100 men, and marching them to this place, viz., Gardiner's Town, which is great dispatch. 21st. All day at Gardiner's Town; weather fine. 22nd. Embarked on board battoes—proceeded up the river toward evening. I lodged at the house of Mr. North, and was very agreeably entertained. 23rd. In the morning proceeded up the river, about six miles, to Fort Western.[50]

Meigs's testimony is crucial to Colburn's case. The landings continued at Colburn's, according to Private James Melvin of Captain Dearborn's company: "Sept. 21, We proceeded up the river s far a the tide would permit and came to anchor within six miles of Fort Western."[51] Lieutenant William Humphrey recorded on September 22, 1775: "This day went on shore to Col. Arnold at Capt. Colburn's. Then there was draughted 110 men to carry out boats to Fort Western; got all things in readiness for proceeding to the above said port."[52] Humphrey left on September 23 but did not complete the move to Fort Western until the end of the twenty-fourth. "This day [24] we were busy'd," he wrote, "in getting our men up, and provisions from Gardinerstown."[53]

The only member of Colonel Enos's company to write anything was Ephraim Squier: "Sept. 22nd, Weighed anchor. Went up to Capt. Cabens[54] nine miles below Fort Western[55] then took battooes along up to Fort Western."[56]

Arnold arrived the evening of Friday, September 21, on the Broad Bay and stayed through Saturday the twenty-third[57] with Reuben and Elizabeth, along with an ambitious upstart: Aaron Burr, in whom Arnold expressed much confidence. They enjoyed the comfort and hospitality of the mansion before the rigors of the trip were upon them. It is a night that cemented the Colburns in history forever.

When the frigates delivered the Continental army to Gardinerstown, they wasted little time changing to the bateaux, even as some of the crafts were still uncompleted. Wrote Justin Smith:

> *Everything looked a-bustle in the shipyard. Colburn himself was on hand, strong and hearty. On hand was Thomas Agry…A squad of workmen were whacking away at their smartest on oars, poles, and paddles, and not far off on the shore lay the fruit of the labor already done—two hundred flat-bottomed boats with high flaring sides, and a rather long, sharp nose at both stem and stern. Arnold came ashore and met with Colburn straight away. "Good day, Colonel Arnold," Colburn said, and saluted.*[58]

Colonel Arnold was a stocky, quick-moving man with bold eyes that burned into people, darting from one issue to another with ease. He immediately surveyed the product. "But Arnold was disappointed with the construction of the bateaux," Smith wrote. "With sides and bottoms made of green pine, the boats were heavy but weak. Many of them appeared to be undersized, and Arnold ordered twenty more to be built within the next week in order to make up for the lost space."[59]

Reuben Colburn likely explained that this was the size of the bateaux used in his area. The concerned Arnold quickly moved on and promised to pay for the additional bateaux to make up the difference. The ever-accommodating Colburn immediately put his partner, Thomas Agry, on the job. This is the source of the alleged £100 payment by Arnold out of his pocket. This author has found no trace of this payment other than a reference in Arnold's correspondence to Washington on September 25, 1775: "The commissary has been obliged to pay for them [the bateaux] with £100 I have lent him out of the pay."[60] Washington never recorded the transaction officially in his books, nor did Arnold list it in his expenses for the expedition.[61]

The crew, however, set to work on these twenty additional bateaux at once, while others loaded bateaux and set out for Fort Western, six miles to the north. Some were transported by wagon to the fort over the course of the next three days. It is certain that business was booming at Henry Smith's Tavern around the first bend in the river from Colburn's, known locally to this day as Smithtown.

Aaron Burr,[62] then just nineteen, had come north from Princeton, New Jersey, where he enjoyed life as the son of the first president of this soon-to-become prestigious college, then the College of New Jersey. He was also a student of law. Burr traveled with his cousin Matthias Ogden, whom Washington had given a captain's commission at Cambridge. Burr would have to prove himself in the field to get his. In the meantime, he would serve as a volunteer cadet. From Newburyport, he wrote to his sister Sally not to worry, that he would become a "papist" after conquering Quebec to win affections of the French girls. Sally knew her brother well. "He intended," young Burr wrote, to return "as sound as I left you in both in the Head & Heart way."

They disembarked at Colburn's from the transport *Sally*. In the course of seeking comforts still available to him, Burr hung around for at least a day, probably longer, as they were assigned to the latter departing regiments before moving on to more comforts from the hospitality of James Howard, commander of the garrison at Fort Western, at his spacious home one mile north of the meager fort at Augusta. In any event, legend has it that Aaron Burr became enamored with Jacataqua, an Abenaki Indian maiden from Swan Island staying at Colburn's with Sabatis and others of the tribes of St. Francis who frequented the Colburn property as Reuben's friends and guests.[63] It is said she became Burr's concubine and faithful servant for the remainder of the trip and longer, or until killed attacking Quebec City. No one knows for sure. If true, this wouldn't have won Burr admiration from the soldiers, who only found hardship, suffering and in many cases death by comparison. The fortunate continued to be so. Like many notables in our history, Burr was a favorite son, an aristocrat, privileged and emboldened by his starting point in life, as are most from similar circumstances.

Colburn's house, a local landmark visible from the river, was a two-story colonial with five fireplaces branching off a central chimney. The windows of the front dining room command a view of the river to the west. The wide boards, milled from trees on Colburn's land, form a wainscot around the room at chair height. When Colonel Arnold, Burr and the officers stayed with Reuben and Elizabeth and dined, the topics of the two evening's conversations are anyone's guess. Oral tradition has it that Arnold was quite taken with Reuben's daughter "Betsey" (his eldest daughter,

Elizabeth), who would have been seven at the time, and he commented on her hair and eyes while bouncing her on his knee before the fire. Reuben also had a daughter Abigail who, at the time of this visit, would have been eight months old and capable of commanding the attention of Arnold and anyone else in the house.

They regaled themselves from the punchbowl in the corner wine closet and ate sumptuous meals at the dining room table. Arnold slept in the northwest corner bedroom upstairs and Burr in the other. In the morning, they attended to the business of moving the vast stores upriver toward Quebec.

Chapter 5

MARCH TO QUEBEC

Arnold carried an address to the Canadian citizens from Washington, imploring them to join the American struggle for independence:

> *Friends and Brethren: The unnatural Contest between the English Colonies, and Great Britain has now risen to such a Height, that Arms alone must decide it…The Hand of Tyranny has been arrested in its Ravages, and the British Arms, which have shone with so much Splendor in every part of the Globe, are now tarnished with disgrace and disappointment…Come then, my Brethren, Unite with us in an indissoluble Union. Let us run together to the same Goal. We have taken up Arms in Defence of our Liberty, our Property; our Wives and our Children: We are determined to preserve them or die…Come then ye generous Citizens, range yourselves under the Standard of general Liberty, against which all the force and Artifice of Tyranny will never be able to prevail.*
> *I am, etc. G. Washington[1]*

Arnold also had a great deal of coinage to pay for any services he might require from the French Canadians, lest the invading army upset the Quebeçois and cause them to lose their neutrality. "In no case were any of the Canadians or their farm animals to be impressed into service."[2]

On the morning of September 23, the troops moved on to Fort Western in waves, while Colburn saw to the construction of the twenty additional bateaux and waited for Commissary Farnsworth and the regiment of

Colonel Roger Enos to arrive. Colburn and his company of artificers would bring up the rear. On September 29, Arnold summoned them forward. "Bring on with you all the carpenters of Capt. Colburn's Company," he wrote to Col. Enos, "and as much provision as the bateaux will carry. When the Indians arrive, hurry them on as fast as possible."[3]

Colburn enlisted the following men to go with him on the thankless detail of maintaining the fleet of bateaux. Nowhere are his brothers mentioned.

Reuben Colburn—Captain, employed from Sept. 13th to Dec. 3rd 1775; Moses Owens—Carpenter, employed from Sept. 20 to Oct. 29th 1775; Dennis Jenkins—Carpenter; Jos. Richardson—Guide; Nath. Evens— Guide; John Door—Carpenter; Daniel Tibbits—Carpenter; Jonathan Weld—Carpenter; James Hill—Guide; Samuel Robbins—Guide; James Does—Carpenter; John Bradley—Guide; Jonathan Scotland—Carpenter; Jos. Webber—Guide; Jos. Davis—Guide, and William North.[4]

In just a few days' time, they would be reviled by the bateaux men, but the complaining never surfaced until years later. The battle with the wilderness to come proved more than enough trouble.

The officers set up command at the Howard home, not the fort itself. So the modern idea that the fort was the headquarters is not accurate. "Headquarters," Dr. Senter noted, "were at Esq. Howard's, an exceeding hospitable, opulent, polite family."[5] Burr may have ridden in the slipstream of Arnold by wagon, declining to man a bateau until forced by necessity. The "lonely" private home was "obliging to a soldier," Burr wrote to Sally of his quarters at Howard's.[6] Fort Western itself was in such a sad condition from lack of use that it wasn't fit to headquarter the expedition, other than a temporary supply stop. "Sept 23rd, Proceeded to Fort Western," wrote Captain Thayer. "This place was formerly pretty strong; was built against the French and Indians, but at present of no great consequence. It has two large and two small block houses."[7]

Colburn joined Arnold and Burr for a celebratory banquet at the private mansion thrown by James Howard, Esq. Kenneth Roberts dismissed this meal as fiction, yet Dr. Senter and others commented on the hospitality offered them by Mr. Howard. The journals place them there at the proper time. Similar treatment was not offered to the infantry, who slept on the ground at the fort in the rain, as Roberts pointed out, as was the experience of Caleb Haskell of Captain Samuel Ward's company. Haskell bypassed Colburn's and disembarked at Hallowell, after a brief stop at

Cobbosseecontee, (Gardiner) before proceeding on foot to Fort Western three miles to the north. "This morning I took my pack, travelled to Fort Weston, where we encamped on the ground. Several of the companies have no tents here," Haskell wrote. "We are very uncomfortable, it being rainy and cold and nothing to cover us."[8]

Our oral family history repeats this banquet tale but carries the story beyond any factual basis, as is often the case with this methodology. This is my great-aunt Bertha's (Major Colburn's great-granddaughter) account of these events in Colburn family tradition. To her credit, Bertha declared that the story was unverified, at least as far as the bear hunting part goes:

> *There is an unverified legend that while Aaron Burr was a guest of Major Colburn, he and a beautiful Indian maiden, Jacataqua, went hunting and brought home a bear and a cub. A great barbecue was held at Fort Western (Augusta) and all of the people round about attended. Colonel Agry[9] from Agry's Point, Squire Oakman,[10] the Major, etc. Burr took Jacataqua to New York and she died later, having borne him a child. Burr was about 19 years of age at that time.[11]*

The Burr fable of providing the bear meat from an encounter in the Howard cornfield—in which he and Jacataqua killed the parents and led the cub back to the fort on a leash—may well be fiction, but the killing and eating of nuisance wildlife is a common practice in rural areas even today. The proposition is not a hard concept to accept. There seems to be no evidence that Burr and Jacataqua had a child together named Chestnutina[12] who later returned to care for him in his last days in New York, but then Burr was also alleged to have fathered President Martin Van Buren, not to mention a host of others. In his last years, Colonel Burr considered these tales to be an honor. But he made a point never to acknowledge these supposed offspring or the women by name.[13] It isn't possible to solve every legendary mystery, particularly specific dialogue attributions and text, except to say that this meal and participants are all but assured to be true based on this analysis. The writers of the journals, as Mr. Roberts has said many times, tended to be terse, inconclusive and selective in what they chose to report. Those who weren't as tight-lipped, like Judge Henry, had an imaginative, embellished recollection:

> *The food consisted of Bear meat, ten baskets of green corn, quantities of smoked salmon, a hundred pumpkin pies, watermelons, and wild*

cherries; and it was eked out by beef, pork, and bread from the military stores. Howard sat at the head of the table with Aaron Burr on his left, splendidly dressed for a wilderness adventure in black knee breeches, blue swallow-tailed coat with gilt buttons, buff vest, silk stockings and silver buckles. Arnold sat at the other end and in between were scattered Major Colburn, who had built the bateaux, Judge Jonathan Bowman, Colonel Charles Cushing, Major Goodwin, the recently converted Tory, and William Gardiner, Esquire.[14]

It was a festive celebration. Henry Dearborn noted such an occasion in his journal entry on September 24, 25 and 26. "We lay at Fort Western preparing for our march," Dearborn wrote. "Fort Western stands on the east side of the river and consists of two Block Houses, and a Large House 100 feet long which are Inclos'd only with Picquets, this House is now the property of one Howard Esq. Where we were well entertained."[15]

Meigs repeats the report of Dearborn with one exception: "Where we were 'exceedingly well entertained.'"[16] This doesn't sound like jerky and sleeping in the rain.

Arnold sent Morgan and the riflemen ahead to clear the road, a testament to the skills he and his men brought to the effort. In addition, a forward scouting party led by Lieutenants Church and Steele and guided by the Getchells embarked for Canada in two birch bark canoes provided by Reuben Colburn.[17] In this party traveled a young John Joseph Henry. "It was concluded," Henry recalled, "to despatch an officer and seven men in advance, for the purpose of ascertaining and marking the paths that were used by the Indians at the numerous carrying places in the wilderness, towards the head of the river; and also to ascertain the course of the river Chaudière."[18]

From Howard's, Aaron Burr sent another letter to Sally that said he was "falling on roast chickens, and wallowing, if you please in a good feather bed." He tried to be reassuring to his concerned sibling, but there seems to be no doubt he was among those given the royal treatment. He doesn't mention either Jacataqua or barbequed bears, but the knowledge of either would have only disturbed her further.

"But adieu to these soft scenes," he wrote. "Tomorrow I traverse the woods. You would laugh heartily to see me accoutred in my travelling dress." He described it for her as a pair of wool trousers over boots and a double-breasted wool jacket topped with a short coat fringed at the belt that he thought curious. On his head sat "a small, round hat with a snap-up brim, topped by a large Fox Tail with a black Feather curl'd up together. The donor I suppose meant to help my deficiency in point of size," he wrote.[19] Aaron Burr was about five feet, six inches. Perhaps he also had a set of dress clothes in addition to this travel outfit. It wouldn't be out of character if he did.

To Commissary Farnsworth, still at Colburn's, Arnold commanded that all the supplies be forwarded to Fort Halifax as soon as possible and the sick returned south on the transport *Broad Bay*: "The goods at Colburn's secure, and leave [there] until the event of the expedition is known. Forward on all the new bateaux, poles oars, pitch, nails, &c. that are or shall be procured, and as soon as you can, join the detachment. Leave particular directions with Mr. Howard to take care of the goods left [at Colburn's]."[20]

The next day, the first wave left Fort Western en route to Fort Halifax in Winslow at the mouth of the Sebasticook River. "Our canoe proved very leaky," wrote Arnold on September 29. At Vassalborough, he exchanged it for a pettigauer, a dugout canoe of sorts, from Remington Hobby.[21] It was an omen of things to come. Others stayed with Hobby as well. "This morning at 10 left F. Western in company with Lieut. Col. Greene, Mr. Burr, and several other gentlemen," wrote Dr. Senter. "Lodged within five miles of Fort Halifax, at Mr. Hobby's."[22] So Aaron Burr rode in Senter's bateau with the medical supplies initially, at the very least, and bunked with him at Hobby's the night after the comforts of Howard's. This puts him at Howard's on the same night for the feast, although Senter never mentions it, as with Dearborn and Meigs.

The Abenaki Indian scout Sabatis was the personal guide for Arnold and his scribe, Adjutant General Captain Eleazer Oswald. Sabatis was a close friend of Colburn, a local hunter and a frequent guest in Colburn's house in Colburntown. A close, friendly relationship with the Indians was a family tradition, and it came in damn handy here.[23] Reuben had been known to say that he preferred Abenaki to the other local help, who gravitated to rum given half a chance, contrary to myth, which would have us believe it to always be the other way around. One can be reasonably assured that both ethnicities were well represented in this attribute, but genetics played a particularly cruel trick on the Indian when it came to the intolerance for distilled spirits, with predictably disastrous results.

The same is true of susceptibility to the Variola virus, the cause of smallpox. But the Abenaki Indians of the Arnold expedition seemed not to be affected, and the soldiers were. This, too, is contrary to the myth that smallpox delivered by the European settlers wiped out American Indians as if on purpose, although there is one case of such a tactic in the French and Indian War employing infected blankets.[24] Biological warfare was a rare tactic, as no one knew of the concept of microorganisms. In fact, centuries of geographic isolation of American Indians, resulting in a lack of resistance to European diseases, was the actual culprit. It is clear no one of that time could have understood this completely. Health was a perilous affair in those days for everyone.

The celebrations behind them, the expedition now began in earnest. As the army passed through what is now Sidney, one of the troops perhaps thought of his legacy and took the time to drill a hole in a rock maple with a hand auger, placing a note in the hole and driving a pine plug to seal the note's tomb—a time capsule.

> *1775 J.B. Dunkirk*
> *with Arnold*[25]

An Augusta sawmill operator found it ninety-two years later while processing a log. The exact number of tree rings in the growth burying it could be counted to the year. Of Dunkirk, nothing further is known.

The bateaux men hadn't gotten very far from Fort Western when a series of falls and rapids extending up the river for half a mile presented an immediate obstacle. "But here, fortunately, a road connected Fort Western and Fort Halifax,"[26] about eighteen miles to the north, at the junction of the Sebasticook and Kennebec Rivers. The local inhabitants made horses and wagons available to help get the heavily laden boats around the falls. Most of the divisions reached Fort Halifax within two or three days after their departure from Fort Western. The time spent at Fort Western was much shorter than the time spent at Colburn's, for the army at least, contrary to conventional wisdom. For Arnold himself, two nights and three days were spent at Colburn's and three at Fort Western. He had a management nightmare to contend with.

Colonel Enos's division, composed of three musket companies plus Colburn's company of carpenters, was slower than the others in getting away from the shipyard, lingering for about a week to move the bulk of the supplies left at Colburn's and the twenty additional bateaux. "To these companies fell all the details common to bringing up the rear of a military column," James Huston of the American Military Institute wrote. "And to forward all remaining supplies to Fort Halifax." To make matters worse, Enos had to "round up the stragglers, arrange for the evacuation of some sick men and one or more criminals."[27]

By September 29, two companies under his command had departed, though Enos himself and Colburn's company of artificers remained behind with Commissary Farnsworth for another day or two. "Arnold remained at Fort Western until the leading companies of the fourth division had set out on the 29th, and then he embarked in a birch-bark canoe paddled by Indians[28] to overtake the head of the column."[29] By the time Dr. Senter, Burr and Greene reached Fort Halifax, their bateau was in trouble: "All our bateaux, camp equipage and c., was carried by hand.[30] By this time several of our bateaux began to leak profusely, made of green pine, and that of the most slight manner. Water being shoal and rocks plenty, with a very swift current most of the way, soon ground out many of the bottoms," Senter wrote.

One could wonder what the already heavy crafts would have been like if the boards had been milled thicker. All but immovable, no doubt. "Saturday, 30th, Ere this, my bateau had arrived at the fort in such a shattered condition that I was obliged to purchase another or not proceed by water without destroying my medicines, stores &c,"[31] he wrote. Dr. Senter bought a seasoned craft for four dollars from an unknown citizen near Fort Halifax and had it transported by wagon upriver.

Ticonic Falls in present-day Waterville is a slate ledge outcropping that spans the river just above Fort Halifax. It forms a barrier but also allows one to walk across the river at this point. That is what the Indians used it for: a bridge of sorts. *Ticonic* or *Taconett* means just that in the Abenaki language. The rapids above here to the town of Fairfield were shallow and rough, causing great problems with the heavily loaded craft. Shoal (exposed sandbars) often grounded the boats like beached whales.

Huston wrote:

> *Beyond Fort Halifax, Ticonic Falls made necessary the first major portage. Already the inexperienced boatmen had found it difficult going to row or pole their bulky craft up the rocky stream, but that was as nothing compared to the work required to get the boats and supplies around such obstacles as this. Still, the expedition was not completely out of touch with civilization, and horses of local inhabitants, as well as a few oxen that were accompanying the expedition, provided some help in the arduous task of portaging the heavy boats and supplies.*[32]

Arnold himself rode by wagon every chance he could get up to as far as Carritunk Falls and stayed in the homes of the Howards, Getchells, Crosiers and the Widow Warren, respectively, as a celebrated guest.

For this long a carry,

> *the bateaux had to be unloaded, the supplies carried to the next launching site, and the boats themselves carried or dragged over the same path. As each boat came to the bank, near the falls, the men would climb out into the water and unload the supplies and equipment; then, passing handspikes [pikes] under the bottom, four men would carry the bulky craft up the bank and around the falls. For shorter distances, and where the banks were not too steep, it was possible to carry the fully laden boat around obstacles without losing time unloading and reloading.*[33]

But the Ticonic Falls were only the first of a series of never-ending falls and rapids where these hand carries, or portages, were necessary. Moreover, in between those that had to be detoured, other, smaller ones joined with boulders, jutting out into the main channel to funnel the swift current so as to put up an "almost continuous battle against the green boats and the green crews."[34] Not far above Ticonic Falls, they had to pole upstream against the "five-mile ripples," carry around Skowhegan Falls and then move along the river again for several miles of boulders and rapids to the difficult portage at Norridgewock Falls.

The weather turned unseasonably cold for late September, and it started to take a toll on the men struggling against the current. The "five-mile ripples" above Ticonic Falls were hard on the bateaux. Already weary, the divisions camped near Pishon's Ferry on both sides of the river and most likely on the island in the middle of the river here. "Dined at Crosier's and hired him with his team to carry over baggage over land about five miles," Arnold recorded on September 30, "to avoid the ripples or quick water above the falls [Ticonic] which are very dangerous and difficult to pass. At 5 p.m. left the landing and proceeded up the river one and one-half miles where we lodged in the woods with Major Meigs & his Division."[35] In the shallows of the river, the heavily laden craft had to be dragged from channel to channel with great difficulty, scraping the pine bottoms clean through, an endeavor that would likely cause the best of us to curse.

Colburn had a "crude" mill in Canaan located just below the island set midstream below the falls, a barrier of considerable consequence, in what is today downtown Skowhegan. By the time the first wave of bateaux approached this bend in the river, they were in dire need of work. Private Morison cursed Colburn, if not by name, but Captain Simeon Thayer, upon seeing the mill, proclaimed in his journal, "Here, there is a mill erecting, (the property of Mr. Copelin),[36] the worst constructed I ever saw. The people call this place Canaan, a Canaan indeed!"[37] Apparently he believed that the concept of a new "Canaan" should be confined to the southern realm of the colony.

That was Thayer's opinion. And it wasn't good. Private George Morison's was worse. "Could we have then come within reach of the villains who constructed these crazy things, they would fully have experienced the effects of our vengeance," he railed. Morison, as Kenneth Roberts noted, was prone to exaggeration and hyperbole. As he approached Canaan, the struggle increased. "Avarice or a desire to destroy us," Morison goes on, "or perhaps both, must have been their motives—they could have had none else. Did they not know that their doings were crimes—that they were cheating their country, and exposing its defenders to additional suffering and death? May heaven reward them according to their deeds."[38]

Morison thought the Colburns were relaxing in the comforts of home and hearth, but in truth, they were following him upriver. While the struggle was real, even bateaux built of seasoned wood would have been torn up dragging over the gravel of the Kennebec in low water conditions, as those found in this particular year. Furthermore, had the pine sideboards been "lapped" over the previous course instead of "butted" flush seam to seam, as some critics[39] have charged,[40] the bateaux would have been more prone to hanging up on rocks and branches. The already worn shoulders of the bateaux men would have been cut to ribbons by the sharp edges. Canoes would have been unable to carry this kind of load and also frequently leaked profusely, as Arnold found out, and later John Henry traveling by such craft with guide John[41] (Jeremiah) Getchell.[42] There was no easy answer to this question, but everyone wanted a scapegoat, both then and now. Even so, there is no mention of confrontation over the builders' work.

Here at Skowhegan Falls, the long, steep portage began in earnest. Everything had to be unloaded and carried over a cliff with a notch to the island's escarpment crest. Food had started to spoil from the leaking casks. In the rear, Colburn's company was starting the journey behind the division of Colonel Roger Enos and had no idea that the need for their services was so great. When he reached his mill at Canaan, Reuben Colburn loaded lumber for the repair job ahead and moved on to the falls. Luckily for him and his crew, the companies ahead of him were too busy to confront him on the so-called faulty construction. Everything came to a head at Norridgewock, where the army stalled, waiting for repairs.

Dialogue between Colburn's artificers and the army that awaited them has not been recorded for posterity. It must have been lively at times. They made the best of it and, like good New England tradesmen, set about the job at hand. Some bateaux were caulked with tar and oakum, and others were partially replaced. Certainly, Washington and Arnold expected problems with the bateaux, or why would they have ordered Colburn to follow with a company of carpenters? Many have second-guessed the use of bateaux on this expedition. John Codman, who died right after writing his lowly regarded version, *Arnold's Expedition to Quebec*, in 1897, suggested that rafts should have been built on-site at the ponds of the Great Carrying Place and beyond. Of course, he went on to refute his own theory and gave the surprise flood most of the credit for the failure of the bateaux. But Arnold's own canoe couldn't make it past Vassalborough without leaking hopelessly. Boat construction is difficult.

The fact remains that some of the bateaux endured all the way to Lake Megantic in the hands of the Virginia Riflemen of Captain Daniel Morgan, as stated above. Some endured and some did not, whatever the reasons might be—the elements, construction, material failure or pilot ineptitude. In any event, the obstacles only increased the farther north they went.

The bedraggled companies, spent from the difficult portage, encamped atop the island, only to awaken with their soaked clothes "frozen a pane of glass thick."[43] They pushed on into the "Bombazee Rips," a long series of rapids between Skowhegan and Norridgewock, so rough that the flotilla was almost completely destroyed. The bateaux were never meant to withstand this kind of punishment and carry these great loads. By the time they reached this point, the seams began to open, and with each new leak, the men violently cursed the boat builders. All attempts to address the leaking by caulking were "only partially and temporarily successful, so that by the time the boats reached Norridgewock Falls, many of the supplies had been ruined, and major overhaul and rebuilding jobs were necessary before many of the craft could proceed any further."[44]

The foodstuffs were carried in wooden barrels and casks of different sizes, so the constant soaking soon had them waterlogged and bursting at the seams, ruining the dried peas and prepared biscuits. It was worse for the stacks of salted fish, most of which were stored in the open and now floated about their feet. "Moreover, the salt beef, prepared during the hot summer, was found to be almost wholly spoiled whether water-soaked or not." The stores of pork fared a little better. "Our fare," wrote Dr. Senter, "was now reduced to salt pork, and flour."[45] There was "little prospect of replenishing supplies before reaching the Canadian settlements, for only two or three families of settlers lived near Norridgewock Falls, and beyond there was nothing but wilderness. Sometimes one of the soldiers was able to bring in a moose, or to catch some fish, but little game stayed near the route of an advancing army."[46] They all hunted, but game was scarce that year, no doubt part of a natural cycle, but a factor nonetheless. The Maine woods were dry that fall of 1775.

Dr. Senter, concerned for his medical supplies, solved the problem in the aforementioned way. There was a great difference in the quality level found in the bateaux on an individual level, as is also the case with men. Daniel Morgan's men managed to pilot their models all the way to the Chaudière River, a further testament to pilot ability as a legitimate determining factor in success.

Arnold arrived on October 2 and remained with the bulk of the forces for a week at the bend in the Kennebec that is the site of the town of Norridgewock. "Here, I overtook Capt. Morgan," Arnold wrote in his journal, "with his division who had just got his baggage over the Carrying Places, which is about 1500 yards over, so high there."[47]

Morgan was sent ahead to cut a trail to the Dead River because his skill as a woodsman and commander warranted him the lead. On October 3, Arnold examined the bread and noted "a great part of which is damaged by the Boats leaking," and lamented Thayer's and Hubbard's companies' difficulty in getting their baggage over the rapids, "where it is impossible for People unacquainted to get up the boats without shipping water."[48]

Captain Reuben Colburn arrived on October 4 with Major Return J. Meigs's division, and the artificers started repairing the bateaux. The companies followed Morgan's lead up and over Carritunk Falls and on to the start of the Great Carrying Place. Arnold traveled by oxcart as far as the trail went, and some of the supplies went with him. The carries around both falls were difficult, and now the army was in the wilderness. By October 9, all had moved on from Norridgewock.

Beyond the point where the Carrabassett River enters the Kennebec, the river changes to a wide but shallow mountain stream. Today, a dam at Bingham (Carritunk Falls) has changed all this and created Wyman Lake, but in 1775, the river would have been what hydrologists would classify as a "large riffle." River bateaux, particularly those heavily laden with casks of meat and flour, weren't meant for this kind of stream travel. Spoilage lightened the load of many bateaux, much to the chagrin of the men in charge. The water washing over the sides was enough to soak and disintegrate the remaining barrels of fish and pork not already spoiled.

The Dead River takes a long northerly course after leaving what is now Flagstaff Lake.[49] It is a wide riffle that can be waded, but the course is miles away from the intended route of the expedition. At a point where a brook flows into the Kennebec on the western bank from the first of three ponds, the army left the main channel and hacked a path to the south shore of First Carry Pond.

> *At ten, arrived at the Great Carrying Place in the river which is very remarkable, a large brook emptying itself into the river just above which comes from the first lake—When abreast of the carrying place in the river, you will observe at about 400 yards above you a large mountain in the shape of a shugar loaf.*
> —*Benedict Arnold*[50]

The brook is large and noisy because it is actually two streams of considerable flow: Carrying Place Stream and North Branch Stream. But it doesn't lead to the first pond directly. The carry is cross-country to the south shore of East Carry Pond, and to the beleaguered members of Arnold's army it must have looked daunting despite the scenic view. It is about a mile and a quarter to the first pond, with what Justin Smith called "a moderate ascent." That's a long way with the load these soldiers had to bear.

"But the wilderness," lamented Private Morison. "Who will ever delight to dwell there? Nature has appointed it for the beasts of the forests and not for man. Dominions are allotted them by a bountiful Giver:—Inhospitable wilds are their domains."[51] Perhaps Morison took precedence as an accidental "divine" conservation advocate, but this is inspired by him being rendered a beast of burden on this march, as was the soldier's position. And the burden was great. "The oppressive weight of our bateaux," he wrote, "the miry state of the earth from rain, the thickets, hills, and swamps were difficulties surmounted with an alacrity that would have astonished the most extensive imagination." Morison, not one to wait for credit where credit was due, declared the effort "the most prodigious march ever accomplished by man."[52] Few would disagree.[53]

It is hard to say how much time they had for fishing, but Arnold mentions "catching a prodigious amount of fine salmon trout" in the first pond. It's not hard to imagine, in 1775, the wilderness lakes teeming with the landlocked version of the Atlantic salmon. The ravenous army certainly needed the nourishment, and more and more succumbed to illness. When they drank the murky water from the smallest of the ponds, Second Carry, dysentery was the result. "A sad plight with the diarrhea," Dr. Senter observed.[54] Many had it already. Arnold decided to build a log hospital in the vicinity of the Third Carry Pond. It is known in the records as "Arnold's Hospital." No trace of it exists today.

> *This day employed Capt. Goodrich's company in building a log house on the 2nd carrying place to accommodate our sick.*
> —*Benedict Arnold, October 12, 1775*[55]

The need for it was dire. Many were infected with smallpox, fatigue, malnutrition, dysentery and, because of the wet, cold weather, severe rheumatism.[56] The water quality in the Second Carry Pond was the culprit in the intestinal woes, being stagnant and "yellow." But injuries also resulted from the "sunken forest," whose knife-like branches hidden in the mud pierced the feet and ankles of the bateaux men on the perilous, torturous carries. Their shoulders were "worn to the bone" in some cases in navigating "The Terrible Carrying Place," as Morison dubbed it.[57]

On October 13, Arnold sent three scouts to carry letters to Quebec City: a white man named Jakins, or Jacquith; and two Indians, one named Eneas and the other unnamed. Some believed, particularly Arnold, that Natanis, who lived in a cabin on the Dead River, was a spy under control of the British. Colburn knew better. Sabatis was a cousin of Natanis (or close friend, related as tribal members are by genetics) but provided no defense for him when Arnold accused Natanis of being a spy based on a misunderstanding of the reporting of Dennis Getchell and Samuel Berry, who scouted the route at Colburn's request before the army arrived.[58] Colburn paid Natanis six shillings as a scout, along with Getchell and Berry, further evidence that he was a known local entity and not the "spy" of record.[59] But Arnold seemed to have just stumbled over this detail without much consideration, as have most of the other writers of this story.[60]

Natanis wisely vacated his cabin on Dead River before the scouting party of Church, Steele and John Henry arrived ahead of the army but took care to leave them a map of the route ahead drawn on a piece of birch bark nailed to a tree. He followed them in the secrecy of the forest, hoping to redeem himself. Eneas, however, never returned, and the British were forewarned, because it was the unknown Eneas who was, in fact, the real spy. The Indian the scouts encountered on the initial scouting trip outlined in the report to Arnold from Getchell and Berry was most likely an unnamed Mohawk sent down from Sartigan. Had Arnold consulted the busy Colburn, laboring behind him, he would have known who the real friend was and thus not be duped, a mistake that bore poisoned fruit in the days ahead.

Those soldiers stuck in the carry and ahead on the Dead River had their hands full. This was the lull before the storm, because little did they know that a rare wandering West Indian hurricane had veered north to meet them. The Third Carry was a dismal swamp described by most participants as "horrendously difficult." The fourth portage was a distance of about three miles from the Third or West Carry Pond to Bog Brook and presented the worst obstacle the troops had encountered to this point.

Beyond a hill near its beginning, this route appeared to be inviting enough—a relatively flat meadow. Carrying the bateaux and supplies for nearly three miles would have been difficult even over hardened grassland, but here the appearance was deceptive. As it turned out, the carry was a tangle of underbrush, moss and marsh.

"While the riflemen of Morgan labored to make some kind of a passable road, the men of Colonel Greene's[61] second division completed the seven or eight trips necessary to get their boats and supplies across, and then they passed through the rifle companies and took the lead in launching their boats down Bog Brook the mile or so to Dead River, and then up Dead River. At first this river was deep and smooth, though the current was strong, but soon rapids again began to force portages."[62] Today, Bog Brook is gone under the waters of Flagstaff Lake.

By now, the wet and cold had taken their toll. Smallpox also stalked them, and many died on the carry. Dr. Senter himself ultimately developed smallpox but survived as he tended to others at the hospital. Bateaux were permanently stationed at each of the ponds to transport the sick and injured back south. Now rations became a problem. So much had been lost getting to this point that the mission was now in peril. Not everybody knew it, and those with the most tended to eat heartily and live in the moment. Others rationed their foodstuffs, as Arnold eventually ordered when he surveyed the situation. Without a doubt, Enos's battalion at the rear was in the best shape. Colburn was in front of him, ferrying supplies, and showed no sign of turning back at this point.

Arnold came up to Greene's division on October 16, in the evening, and Greene wasted no time informing his commander that he was indeed short of food. In fact, they had taken to boiling candles as a thickener for the hot water soup. Arnold was immediately concerned and dispatched Major Bigelow[63] with two groups of twenty-nine privates to return to the rear and help forward up the supplies. They left immediately. Bigelow carried with him a letter to Enos from Arnold. "The whole having only four barrels of flour and 10 bbls. of pork," he wrote assessing the supplies at the Greene camp. Arnold ordered Enos to give as much of his stores, particularly flour, as he could. He further added, "If your men are much fatigued and this party [Bigelow and company] can bring more provision than their share; let them have It;—you shall have it again when you come up, and it will forward the whole. The carpenters of *Colburn's company* have more than they can bring up."[64]

Goodrich, Dearborn and Meigs arrived at the Greene camp on October 18 and pushed on the next day. The rains came in the night and stayed for three days. This location was somewhere below Eustis at the base of Mount Bigelow. Thayer determined the mountain to be "6 miles S.E. by E." The camp was about four miles beyond the cabin of Natanis, described by Thayer in passing as an "Indian hut where one Sataness, dwell'd, both as rogueish and malicious as ever existed."[65] The area is in the middle of what is now Flagstaff Lake, formerly Flagstaff Village. By the time Colburn and company arrived at the Greene camp the flood caught them, along with the companies of Thayer and Topham, who had been passing the time making "cartouches" as Arnold instructed.[66] Enos still trailed his advance companies back at Bog Brook. By this time, Arnold, having thought he'd attended to the dire conditions at the Greene camp, was camped on the Dead River somewhere above the present town of Eustis when the river rose eight feet overnight at a place Arnold described as "30 miles from Chaudiere Pond."[67] Smith figures this is one mile above Ledge Falls.[68] The river rose so fast that at "4 o'clock in the morning Arnold and his party were awakened by a rush of waters, and before they could remove their baggage it was all in the flood."[69] "The extreme rains and freshets in the river have hindered our proceeding any farther," Arnold penned from his portable writing desk to Enos the next day.[70]

At the Greene Camp, Bigelow returned with only two barrels of flour. The officers of Enos's company—and for a brief time Enos himself—who expected to find Arnold, followed. Disappointed, Enos returned to "drive up his rear." "Now, we found ourselves in a distress'd and famish'd situation," Thayer wrote, "without provisions and no hopes of getting any, until we reached Sartigan."[71]

Having no other choice, Thayer and eight men pushed north but became lost in a freshet of floodwaters that required they wade through waist-deep water and drag their bateaux for the rest of October 22, remaining without "victuals and water until 9 o'clock the next morning."[72] They reached a detachment about to begin their march. This would be Greene's forward progress. They all continued on for several miles up a rising Dead River above Eustis. Snow plagued them and left the struggling army "in a situation not to be described." And yet they forged ahead "against a very rapid stream." At an undisclosed location "25 miles from the Height of Land," according to intelligence Thayer records receiving, they learned just how difficult a path lay before them. Thayer and company moved on for three more miles and encamped while waiting for their boats. Greene had hoped to find Arnold, but he was far ahead, and now Greene had to deal with the discontentment of his starving troops, who were reduced to eating boiled candles and pieces of leather. "We are in absolute danger of starving, however I hope for the best," Captain Topham wrote.[73] Greene had to solve the conundrum of what should they do now.

> *Here Col. Greene, Capt. Topham and myself staid, by desire of Col. Enos to hold a council of war.*[74]

There were two councils of war held here on the Dead River. The first as an army, consisting of Greene, Topham, Thayer, Bigelow and Hubbard, voted for both divisions moving forward. Enos and his men would stay the course and suffer the same fate as the others. Enos cast the deciding vote to continue on, but his captains—McCobb, Williams and Scott—Adjutant Hyde and a Lieutenant Peters didn't like the outcome of the first council and held another among themselves, deciding to return south with the supplies.[75] Enos then decided that his allegiance lay with his division. Thayer, enraged (with good reason), asked for some supplies so they could continue, and they granted the request. It was determined that Thayer would return to the rear of the column and procure some of their supplies, as his own had been lost in the floodwaters. He says he now had to have a bateau to retrieve them and had trouble convincing Colburn to give him one for the trip downstream on October 25. The reason is unclear. Captain Thayer, who seemed to have ill feelings for Reuben Colburn from the start, now complained about him some more.[76] Thayer was not one to quibble with when it came to the subject of military courage; he had plenty to spare and was sorely tested here, but his contempt for Colburn seems unjust in retrospect.

> *To which we replied if thus determined to grant us some supply, which they promised, if we could get a boat from Mr. Copelin* [Colburn] *tho' with ye utmost reluctance.*
> —*Captain Simeon Thayer*[77]

The result is that Colburn *did* give him a boat, and Captain Thayer and Matthias Ogden (sans Aaron Burr) left on a fast ride down the river to get the flour and pork. Who knows the reasons for Colburn's reluctance? Maybe it was his personal bateau that Colburn's life depended on. Maybe it was one of the few that still floated; we don't know. The implication is that he was stingy and uncooperative. Colburn and company had to press on to Canada, and his remaining bateaux were crucial to his part of the mission. It was important to look out for number one should Colburn live up to his part of the bargain. He had promised Washington he would see them through. The Enos company gave Thayer only two barrels of flour, half what was promised, when he finally caught up with them. He was, in his words, "utterly deceived." When informed of his officers' decision to return to Cambridge, Enos agreed and ordered the division to turn back. Then, somewhat reluctant, he bid Thayer "a tearful farewell."[78] Thayer, cursing "the ill-hearted minds of the timorous party," and Ogden struck out with the two barrels of flour and the boat "working against a most rapid stream"[79] for miles, having to spend the night in the snow without shelter. They overtook their troops the next morning and pushed on to the Height of Land.

This is the last evidence we have of the Colburn company on the march to Quebec. Where did they go and when? It would seem the carpenters of Colburn's company were for all practical purposes out of work at this point. I am skeptical that they did an immediate about-face such as described by the lone journalist from Enos's company, Ephraim Squier, a private in Scott's company: "We marched till 2 o'clock in the afternoon [October 25] then was ordered to march back to our camp. The Colonel gave orders this morning that as many as had a mind return, and seven out of a company must return."[80] Squier reports this location is somewhere on the Dead River. He reached Bog Brook on October 18, and the rain continued for three days. "Hard for poor soldiers to have to work hard in the rains and cold, and to wade a mile and a half knee-deep in water and mud, cold enough, and after night to camp in the rain without any shelter."[81] They built a fire, but the rising water forced them to retreat in the night. "The river raised, we judge, 12 feet, so windy that it was dangerous to be in the woods." Following his orders to return, Squier reports using bateaux to return south with stores of gear and provisions for two days per man for those going by land and by water from Bog Brook on.[82]

This places Colburn and the rest of the divisions far up the North Branch Dead River, well on their way to Chain of Ponds. Thayer confirms this. I see the Colburn company pressing on, doing what they could for the success of the mission. But with the ill will of many of the soldiers due to the faults of the bateaux, who could blame them for quitting? After all, the Colburn company of carpenters was in no way required to attack Quebec but only to support the trip logistically and in maintenance. They did that. With mass starvation looming ahead and many sick and injured to return to the settlements, for them there was no disgrace in going home at this point. But they didn't. Not so for the companies of Colonel Roger Enos.

On the upper North Branch Dead River, in the wake of the flood, a young John Joseph Henry, traveling with guide John Getchell, found his party's canoes pierced by snags, torn open amidships and folded in half by the rapid current. "Quick as lightening," Henry recalled decades later, "that side of the canoe was laid open from stem to stern, and water was gushing in upon us that would have inevitably sunk us in a second of time, but for that interference of Providence which is atheistically called presence of mind."[83]

Henry was prone to over dramatization, but the proper attribution has to go to Getchell. This Getchell,[84] John, the brother of fellow scouts Dennis[85] and Nehemiah Getchell of Vassalborough, an especially ingenious woodsman, sent Henry and an Irish guide into the woods for cedar roots and birch bark while he searched for turpentine in its raw form—pine pitch. Once found, the crew watched intently while Getchell set about stitching up the gaps in the birch bark craft by the fire, sealing the repairs with the mixture of pitch and grease from an empty leather pork bag. Underway again, to their dismay, the whole affair reoccurred, and the repairs had to be repeated. So our canoe crews had their own navigation problems as well, but with the expert guidance of Reuben Colburn's scouts, the army got through, if not unscathed.

Major Meigs paid the scouts, Nehemiah Getchell and Samuel Berry, at the Height of Land: Seven-Mile Stream (Arnold River, to be exact),[86] their mission completed once the expedition reached Canada. If Colburn and his carpenters didn't make it this far, they were close. And that is the logical end for them as private citizens.

Henry Dearborn testified to Congress in the legal fight in 1818 that Colburn went to "the headwaters of the Kennebec." Since it is unlikely that meant Moosehead Lake, it must have meant the Dead River at the Chain of Ponds. At least that's my contention. The exact point of the about-face is unclear.[87] Did Colburn turn around with Enos after his defection? Mr. Smith asserts that he did. "The family tradition has it Colburn returned with Enos," Smith wrote. "This seems every way probable, and agrees with

Dearborn's statement."[88] No, it doesn't. Dearborn asserts that Colburn pushed on. Family tradition didn't even have Reuben on the march.

It is doubtful that he returned with Enos, as Colburn was instructed to assist the entire expedition, not any one company. Colburn took no orders from Enos. His allegiance was to Washington and Arnold, not subordinates. It seems likely that when the need to repair bateaux was over, so was his mission. Moreover, the point of Enos's return was far from the headwaters of the Dead River many miles back near Eustis, so this doesn't agree with Dearborn's statement. The point of return for the Colburn company was most likely somewhere near the head of the Dead River at the Chain of Ponds just below the height of land at the Canadian border. From there, snow falling and with untold horrors in their recent memory (and much more ahead for the army), Colburn and his carpenters floated downstream in bateaux that had brought them there and now would take them back home.

Chapter 6

INTO THE SWAMPS OF CHAUDIÈRE POND

G uided by Colburn's scouts, the divisions moved on after the flood as best they could. Arnold made it to the first of the Chain of Ponds on October 25 "quite early in the forenoon."[1] It was blustery and snowing. The night before, it "rained and snowed all night," Arnold wrote.[2] Arnold's party rowed two miles where the lake narrowed before opening up for the same distance, ending in a "marshy ground." After a mile of river, he came to another pond "about five miles long."[3] The lakes are Lower, Bag, Round, Horseshoe and Moosehorn.

"All these lakes are surrounded within a chain of prodigious high mountains," he wrote.[4] As they struggled from pond to pond and into Horseshoe Stream, the wind and snow continued to pound them. "In the last lake the sea ran so high we were obliged to go on shore to bail our battoes, which was with much difficulty kept above water."[5] Heavily laden and in high, windblown waves, it's hard to imagine a craft that could have accomplished this trip without difficulty. They had to search hard for the portages and cut their way through piles of drift logs, becoming soaked and nearly frozen in the process.

On October 26, Arnold came to the end of Moosehorn Pond that now bears his name and the start of the carrying place over the Height of Land and into Chaudière Pond. The country was hellish, with great swaths of blow-downs they had to skirt and then return to the course; mire holes, swamps, treacherous bogs and thickets where dead twigs snap into one's eyes; precipices and ravines.[6]

Arnold climbed the portage much the worse for wear and worried about those behind him. At the top was "a beautiful meadow." Here, he ran into twenty of the advance men from Lieutenant Church and Steele's company. While they continued to ferry up the gear over the portage, Arnold sent back Nehemiah Getchell, another of Colburn's scouts, to see the rest through.[7]

The food situation would, of course, become dire or even deadly for some. Greene's division was already boiling moose hide shot pouches at their camp below present-day Eustis. Arnold by this time was over the height of land and had sent Captain Oliver Handchitt ahead to Quebec with orders to procure supplies from the Canadians, but he soon passed him. He sent Isaac Hull,[8] one of Colburn's scouts with Getchell and Berry,[9] back to those waiting in the meadow with the instructions, but it did no good, because the message missed[10] some of the men who already had set out. These were Dearborn's, Goodrich's, Smith's and Ward's companies.[11] Hull was to guide the fourth division in the rear after delivering the message, but they retreated before he arrived.[12]

The ordeal by Lac Megantic was close to horrific. Division after division became mired and ultimately lost in myriad channels, miles of blown-down spruce and swamps of the Arnold (Seven-Mile Stream) and Spider Rivers. Arnold had warned of this, but his message wasn't heeded. "This error was occasioned by their endeavoring to keep to the stream," Arnold wrote, "whereas they should be from the carrying place kept on the high land."[13] Arnold was using *Montresor's Journal*, but that journal makes no mention of the swamps that were now engulfing the troops.[14] Indeed, he had to rescue Handchitt and company himself from the bog.[15] "I immediately sent all the Battoes for them," Arnold wrote upon discovering their plight.

It took several trips in bateaux to rescue more than sixty men. Notably, the now infamous Colburn bateaux were still in service, but many of the travelers perished in the swamp. The other woman on the expedition— besides Jemima Warner, seventeen—was Susannah Grier, wife of Private Joseph Grier, a hefty woman who commanded the men to "avert their eyes as she hiked up her skirts" to wade across the streams and fought on with her husband in the battle to come. Arnold raced ahead with hopes of reaching Sartigan and procuring the much-needed supplies, but this proved more difficult than he could imagine even at this point in the ordeal.

On October 27, Arnold reached the Chaudière River on the north side of the lake, where he met with Lieutenants Steele and Church. He decided to take fifteen men in four bateaux down the river and procure the supplies.

A forward scout reported that the inhabitants were "rejoyced to hear we are coming,"[16] Arnold wrote. The bateaux were still in good service and remained a key element in whatever success might lie ahead for the army. Arnold predicted this effort would take him three days, all of which would be by water.

The adept Arnold negotiated the swamp with great expertise for a non-woodsman Connecticut trader and made a great attempt to pass on this insight from his experience to those behind him. "You must all of you keep to the east side of the lake," he wrote. "You will find only one small river until you reach the crotch which is just above the inhabitants."[17] Arnold meant Sartigan, which was jumping the gun at this point for the others, who were still struggling to find the lake. He hoped to have the supplies back up the river in six days' total time. Then, in an indication of the peril they all were in, he wrote: "Pray make all possible despatch."

Matthias Ogden, Burr's cousin, wrote on October 27:

> *This day we were employed in transporting our boats to the river leading to Chaudier Pond*[18] [Seven-Mile Stream, i.e., Arnold River]. *The land raises gradually about half the distance across the portage, where we were we all much pleased in seeing the brooks running north, which was our direct course. After finishing our portage the provision belonging to the whole was collected and equally divided among the whole regiment. We shared about □ of a pound of pork per man and five pints, scant measure, of flour which was to last us [reaching] the inhabitants. The riflemen were wholly destitute of any kind of meat before this for eight days.*[19]

Ogden goes on to cite receiving the letter from Arnold:

> *At four o'clock in the afternoon we heard a shout from the men near the river, which soon reached throughout camp. We received a letter from Col. Arnold informing us of the return of the two Indians, from whom he received an answer to his letter to Quebec, informing him that the inhabitants were much rejoiced at our near approach, would assist in repulsing the King's Troops there and forever go hand in hand with us.*[20]

Not quite, since Eneas, one of the Indians, also informed the British of the impending attack, which was his mission from the outset and his first contact with the expedition at Norridgewock. The inhabitants, the French, were indeed helpful to the cause. The letter instructed the army on which course to take to avoid the swamp maze and make it into the lake. "He directed us to take a northeast course from the height of land, which would bring us to the Chaudier River and beyond."[21]

Speaking of Goodrich's forward party: "The remainder (of the troops) belonging to the boats, about ten in number, had orders to set off by daylight and wait for the arrival of the landmen at the entrance of the Chaudier. Col. Arnold informs us likewise that in six days he will meet us with provisions."[22] A long six days it would be.

Goodrich commandeered Ogden's bateau. "In the morning, being disappointed in my boat that was taken back by the express sent by Col. Arnold, Col. Green sent back word that I might send back the boat's crew belonging to the Company and take her myself."[23] He did and set out with "Messrs. Burr (Aaron), Melcher and a Lieut. belonging to Capt. Thayer."[24] "We followed a small stream which in about ten miles led us to Amegunti Lake or Chaudier Pond."[25] For Ogden and company, there were no lost days in the swamp since they heeded Arnold's instructions. The bateaux were still functioning at this point and were a key element to the advancement of the army.

Ogden, Burr and company reached the lake and steered northeast, overtaking Morgan and Smith at the "bark house." They moved on to the head of the lake sixteen miles hence, according to Ogden. He reports they missed the river and encamped anyway. Seeing the smoke, Morgan, Smith and Ward joined them for the night.[26]

On October 28, Henry Dearborn came upon Captain Goodrich, who had been wading around in the swamps of the Spider River for a day trying to find a way across without boats.[27] Apparently his were out of service at this point. As they found out the hard way, this was no place to be without a watercraft. The channel is braided and deep. Goodrich was nearly frozen up to his armpits and holed up on an island in the channel when Dearborn and a Mr. Ayres[28] came downstream in a canoe. His company soon arrived and contemplated building a raft, but Dearborn had them hold off while he searched for a crossing point. Goodrich wasn't so sure and determined that no clear way had appeared to him to get to the pond from where they now were. It was a major morass.

One of the sergeants was ill and had gone on in a canoe looking for the right channel, and Goodrich had no idea what his fate was. This was James Grier and his wife, Susannah. Finally, Dearborn and Goodrich emerged into the lake and came upon the bark house camp established by Morgan and his men in the first wave. One man remained behind to inform the rest of the progress. After looking ahead in hopes of finding the missing bateau, they spent an uneasy night and then went back in the morning to ferry across the straggling company. Getting them across the two rivers took the better part of the day, and soon all were at the bark house still worse for wear, not to mention hungry. That was never-ending.

Dearborn moved on the next day to the mouth of the Chaudière River, still traveling with Ayres. His company arrived and proceeded down the river, but Dearborn walked eight miles and complained of not feeling well. He camped by a waterfall. Ten bateaux had capsized on the run, all except for Dearborn's and Arnold's. Ayres must have been the pilot of the former and rode with Private James Melvin,[29] one of the journalists. As usual, Arnold slid through every obstacle unscathed. One man (George Innis)[30] drowned on this last leg, and they piled up at this point on the Chaudière, not known as the "boiling cauldron" for no reason.

Back in the swamp, stragglers remained mired in and lost. As they struggled to find the lake, Dearborn patched his canoe and ran thirty miles of rapids and falls that he expected to have "stove her to pieces."[31] Now, with the canoe completely in tatters, he walked ashore and encamped. What he found was shocking. Some of the footmen sat in camp, gaunt and almost starved. "This day Capt. Goodrich kill'd my dog, and another dog, and eat them," he wrote. "I remain very unwell."[32] Dearborn could find no reason or the strength to protest.

Ogden and Burr came upon this camp a day later on October 30. "After traveling a short distance we came upon Capt. Goodrich's track, which soon led to where he encamped the evening before. We here found," Ogden wrote, "a part of two quarters of dog they had killed and hung up for the remainder of his Company that was behind; the other they had eaten and taken with them. One of our Company, rejoiced to find the prize, immediately cut a part of it, roasted it on the coals, and ate very greedily."[33]

"About an hour after," Ogden continued, "we fell in with the rest of the Company which had passed another way. We found them much dejected and spent with fatigue and hunger. We informed them of the meat, at which they sent two men for it immediately."[34]

Later, at three o'clock in the afternoon, they hailed Captain Dearborn and a companion going downstream in a birch canoe. Dearborn told them Morgan had "his boat split upon a rock, and most of his effects, lost, and one man drowned."[35] He reports that they also saw Arnold's wrecked boat but didn't know what was lost from that incident. Ogden and company marched twenty more miles and camped, fatigued and hungry.

The next day, November 1, they continued on for two hours until they came upon a smashed canoe pinned against a rock in midstream. Ogden supposed it to be Dearborn's. At two o'clock, they came upon a man lying beside the trail who belonged to Goodrich's company. He hadn't eaten in three days, he said, and "was too spent to proceed." Ogden pitied the man, giving him a full half of his pork, which only amounted to two ounces. Captain Smith gave him half of his bread, which he wolfed down immediately. "He was so refreshed," Ogden wrote, "that he came on with us."[36]

They made twenty-two more miles and camped at sunset, when they shared a "bit of chocolate equally in spoonfuls." The journey was made more difficult for Ogden by his boots being completely worn out. He had covered them with a piece fashioned from a flour sack, but it was worn out as well, and his feet suffered for it. He wasn't alone in that complaint.

Carrying on, on the morning of November 2, they awoke and marched eight more miles until, as if in a dream, five horned cattle appeared before them, accompanied by two canoes full of mutton: the supplies sent by Arnold. "No sensation could be equal to it," Ogden wrote.[37] "Welcome to Canada," the Frenchmen told them. They feasted on the spot and then moved on to join the rest of the regiment at Sartigan (St. Georges).

For the others, an equally harrowing ordeal was still in progress. "We wandered for three days," Dr. Senter wrote. "Our main course was W.N.W. and only varied to escape the bogs, mountains, small ponds, water streams, &c., of which we met with many."[38] His companions had long given up hope of arriving at the destination and felt that they would not even recognize it should they succeed. Soon, while taking turns with the compass with Colonel Greene, they struck a course due west and found the lake. Eventually, they wound up at the fall with the rest, including Morgan, who led the initial run down the Chaudière with disastrous results.

On the island in the Spider Swamp, Jemima Warner, traveling with her husband, James, ran into terminal problems described by Abner Stocking as a "victim to the king of terrors."[39] When he succumbed to what must have been a combination of ailments and starvation, his bereft young wife buried him with leaves and waded off toward Quebec with her musket raised high, keeping her powder dry. Twenty miles later, she caught up with Stocking's company. For her and many others, it was a death march.

When Captain Jonas Hubbard's company wandered into the same swamps of Spider Lake, they expected to walk through with little trouble. While snow and rain fell, with the food down to five pints of flour and a piece of pork, the company increasingly worried that it had taken a wrong turn. It had. Just when hope had dwindled to the lowest point, a male Indian emerged from the forest and strode into the dismal camp. Natanis, the falsely accused spy, had been keeping an eye out for them and now was compelled, at his own risk, to reveal himself. It is unclear why Arnold chose to believe the wrong man. Eneas had betrayed him earlier, tipping off the British, but now Natanis the savior received his redemption.[40]

He had "some practical knowledge of the country," Fobes noted. "Under his directions, after another day's fatiguing march, we reached the banks of the Chaudière: thus accomplishing in three days what might have been done in less than two if we had not missed our course."[41]

This is yet another indication of the skill of Reuben Colburn and his scouts in the face of the ineptness, if not incompetence, of the troops insofar as wilderness skills are concerned. Even with Reuben and the others now gone back, his instructions remained in effect. Few European settlers had the diplomatic skills with the native Abenaki that Colburn did. With the rescue fairly successful, they moved on down the river hoping to meet up with Arnold or those carrying provisions from the French settlement.

Surveyor John Pierce, traveling with Lieutenants Steele and Church on October 22, his birthday, said goodbye to his "pilot-Getchel," who returned home on this day.[42] This would be John Getchell. On October 25, Pierce reported seeing "smook" in the distance.[43] Fearing Indians and the British, they spent an uncomfortable night in the snow and rain. In the morning, they found Handchitt and company down in the Spider and spent grueling hours up to their armpits in water trying to find the lake. Initially, they failed and built five fires trying to warm themselves. Two men swam across the channel and found Arnold, who hadn't left down the Chaudière yet, and he sent the aforementioned rescue by bateaux to ferry them over. Pierce was a good hunter and killed twelve partridges while he waited for passage.

On October 28, he still complained of meager rations and disaster twelve miles down the rock-strewn river. Here, "my boat ran against a rock," he wrote, "and the man in the bow, Cyrus Stebbins, pitched over but kept hold of ye bateau as she lay broadside to ye water, he with some difficulty got her off and went on his course another ten rods when she struck another rock and knocked out the man, O. Smith." He swam to shore just as they drove the bateau ashore and abandoned the watercourse for the land option.[44] Considering what happened to Arnold's crew, it was probably a wise choice.

Arnold was close to his immediate goal on October 30, when, after negotiating a set of rapids the day before, they filled another bateau with water but luckily "lost nothing."[45] "Here," he wrote, "we were obliged to lower down the stream by our painters: lower we came to a falls." The "painters" could be remnants of the Colburn company of carpenters and caulkers. After the falls and a short portage, Arnold met two Penobscot Indians who "appeared friendly and assisted us over the portage." Seven miles later, four beyond the confluence of the Des Loups, they saw the first house. Arnold was mistaken, as he's describing the *Liniere* entering present-day St. Georges. He was relieved to have made it, but now attending to the failing army at his rear was paramount, should the effort still have a chance.

Unfortunately, Arnold's journal beyond this point was never found, but his letters remain. He was a prolific letter writer with a traveling desk that he set up no matter how bad the terrain and conditions were at the time. Once encamped in Sartigan, he quickly penned a letter to all of the officers:

> *I have now sent forward for the use of the detachment 5 bbls and 2 tierces and 500 lbs. Of flour by Lt. Church, Mr. Barrin and 8 Frenchmen, and shall immediately forward on more, as far as the falls. Those who have provisions to reach the falls will let this pass on to the rear; and those who want, will take sparingly as possible, that the whole may meet with relief. The inhabitants received us kindly and appear friendly in offering us provisions, & c. Pray make all possible despatch.*
> *I am gent. Your's &c. B. Arnold*[46]

On November 1, Pierce made it to the falls, where he found Wesson and Stebbins. Together, they went two miles downriver before running into "Lt. Church and three Frenchmen with 5 cattle, 2 horses, 2 sheep, 11 bushels of flour."[47] They had eaten all of their provisions by then and had killed and eaten one of their dogs at twelve o'clock. That night, Pierce, who had a habit of hunting well in the wild and in town, dined with the Indians and bought "20 Lbs of butter for the detachment." He was "treated very kindly this night," he wrote, and "slept between two Frenchmen in a French house—it was very odd to hear them at their devotion." I'll leave the exact meaning of his observation to the reader. When he moved on the next day, a "fat beef" was killed and mutton and eggs bought before he stayed at a tavern with as much French brandy as he could hold at his disposal. For Pierce, things were looking up.

Likewise for Dr. Senter, who found the devouring of the same dog (Dearborn's Newfoundland) unnerving and "without leaving any vestige of the sacrifice."[48] Nor did the other pitiful fares sampled at the falls: "Shaving soap, pomatum, and even lip salve, leather of their shoes, cartridge boxes

&c."[49] Then, on November 2, the surreal visages of horned cattle appeared before the starving soldiers. And they were real to the joy of all present. "Echoes of gladness resounded from front to rear!" he wrote. "Capt. Topham and I shed tears of joy in our happy delivery from the grasping hand of death," wrote Captain Simeon Thayer.[50]

At St. Mary's, Arnold bought a team of oxen and left them for Pierce to employ or eat as he saw fit. He was to wait and see to the need of the straggling troops who started to come in slowly: "All wont shoes and many clothes—The French grow very dear."[51]

Chapter 7

POINT LEVIS

Mathias Ogden met Arnold in St. Francisway above Sartigan after being satiated with the provisions sent. Arnold said he was highly received by the inhabitants, who told him "they imagined he was sent from heaven to restore them liberty, and rang the parish bell on the occasion."[1] Arnold arranged a meeting with Indians of the different tribes who wanted to know the nature of the "quarrel with the King and his children."[2] After Arnold informed them on the particulars, they were willing to go with the army and "fight anybody who should molest us." They wanted bread for themselves and their children in return and refused to be in any garrison. Arnold signed them up at eight dollars per month and gave them a two-dollar advance against those wages.

At Sartigan, the once hunted Natanis approached Lieutenant Steele and shook his hand in a manner "intimating a previous knowledge of him," Henry wrote.[3] He was with the group of Indians at the meeting, after delivering the lost companies from the swamps, when Steele asked Natanis why he hadn't come forward sooner. "You would have killed me," he told Steele.[4] Arnold rushed forward and demanded an explanation, too, and was equally surprised at his misjudgment but relieved. And now in the company of the other Abenaki and Paul Higgins, who had gone with Colburn at his request to Cambridge in August, the allegiance was clear once and for all.[5] Natanis was accepted at last into the Continental fold and marched with the leading companies toward Point Levis.

Arnold gave Burr a new job: sending a message to General Montgomery disguised as a priest. "In this order of men he was willing to repose confidence."[6] A priest with whom Burr confided attempted to dissuade them from proceeding with the attack and spoke of it as "impossible to accomplish."[7] But he admired young Burr's resolve and obtained him a guide and a cabriolet (sleigh) for snow travel and went from one Catholic house to another before holing up for three days in a convent, where rumors of Arnold's arrival spread through the village. Eventually, he was slipped out of town and reached Montgomery in Sorel, where he became his aide-de-camp. Fortune smiled on Mr. Burr once more.

Ogden continued downriver in a new canoe and, at St. Marie, was informed that Guy Carleton had taken the Indian express sent by Arnold to the city and held him prisoner. Conflicting accounts further added to the confusion over the state of affairs in Quebec, but Ogden deduced that since the first dispatch sent with Eneas back at Norridgewock, no word had come back to them, and subsequent messengers simply disappeared. The "Indian's express had betrayed us," he wrote, "and given up our letters."[8] There was nothing to do except move on.

In a falling snow on a muddied road, they were slogging toward St. Andrew when they came upon two well-mounted Frenchmen who told them a number of citizens in Quebec were under arms but would lay them down when the army arrived.

On November 7, they marched into St. Auree, where further investigation revealed the two men were spies. They waited here for the rest to come up, and Arnold sent a party of thirty men on to Point Levis to determine the true nature of what they faced. A twenty-six-gunship patrolled the harbor. "Our situation now seemed somewhat ticklish," Ogden wrote. "As yet we had no certain intelligence of the strength of the enemy at Quebec, nor had we heard a word from general Schuyler or his army."[9]

The army now numbered 600 out of the 1,100 who had started from Cambridge in September, "and they were not all effective; the most of us naked and barefoot and very illy-provided with ammunition; the winter approaching in hasty strides and we had no quarters we could call our own, nor any possibility of retreating, but by fighting our way to Gen. Schuyler, with a handful of men, through all of Carleton's army."[10]

On November 8, this gloomy mood was broken by the arrival of a sentinel who alerted that two Indians were on express from General Montgomery, which "gave us new life and lifted our spirits."[11] Major Timothy Bigelow reported that British regulars had burned three houses and cut sixty boats to pieces to prevent Arnold's army from landing at Point Levis for crossing to Fort Quebec, thus undermining an advance already in serious jeopardy from nature itself.

Having been told by two Frenchmen that the boats had been destroyed at Levis to prevent their crossing, Colonel Greene returned to the rear to get as many canoes as were left and proceed on to Point Levis with the remaining divisions. The French came through with fleets of birch canoes, and the bells in the mass house were set to ringing upon hearing who the travelers to their land were. It was the start of an invaluable alliance in the Revolutionary War.

To further complicate matters, two British gunboats had arrived on the scene to try to prevent a crossing. Fobes speaks of the "sloop of war" stationed upriver. Ogden arrived at noon, traveling twelve leagues, and found a full view of the harbor containing one frigate of twenty-six guns and one sloop of war of sixteen guns, called the *Hunter*, besides several small cutters.

As John Pierce was amply entertained all the way down the lower river, the hobbled, mostly barefoot army struggled to follow. Slowly they did though, and on November 9, Pierce and company arrived by canoe at Point Levis. Hubbard's company made it on November 11. According to Simon Fobes of that company, they didn't attempt to cross until November 20.[12] "Here we were made to halt, and quartered with the inhabitants about two weeks," he wrote.[13] As with Pierce, the French made every effort to make them as comfortable as possible. They busied themselves building ladders and fashioning spears to assault the walls of the city.

During this time, there came an American businessman by the name of Halstead who had evacuated the city and taken his family to the Island of Orleans. Although his knowledge of conditions in the city was limited, it was better than what they had. The frigate was from London, arriving from St. John's, and carried on it "150 recruits and landed 50 marines and these, with about 100 Tories, and 200 Canadians were all within the walls of the upper town."[14] He said they would probably lay down their arms under attack, and the Indian express (Eneas) had given the letters to the enemy. The intended recipient, Mr. Mercier, was taken prisoner onboard the frigate without being informed as to why.

When a boat embarked from the sloop across to a gristmill, the alarmed colonials went to engage it in battle, but the attempt failed, and one man was captured and taken prisoner back to the camp.[15] On November 13, news came by way of a French inhabitant that the Indian carrying the letters to Montgomery had been captured by three men on war boats coming from Montreal, but one had escaped and gotten through. "Lucky for us," Ogden wrote.[16]

Arnold held a council and informed the captains of each company to prepare for the crossing at once. It wasn't clear if, upon arrival, they should storm the city or wait. The council decided to leave that decision up to Colonel Arnold. Now he had to prepare for the crossing, and as usual, the weather wasn't cooperative, with high winds howling up the flat valley.

With the canoes now assembled from the rear and other villages, they began the crossing in waves, since there still weren't enough bateaux to hold all the soldiers. "At about eleven o'clock on the night of November 13 the crossing began," Huston wrote.

> *By four o'clock the canoes had made three round trips in the quiet darkness, carrying some 500 men across the mile-wide river. The rest of the force, excepting sixty men who remained on the south bank as a rear guard, followed the next night or two. Of the approximately 1,050 officers and men who had left Cambridge, approximately 675 had arrived at the St. Lawrence River and the gates of Quebec. If 300 returned back with Enos, there were only about seventy-five casualties and stragglers who failed to come through the whole ordeal.*[17]

"At eight in the evening the first load for the canoes embarked," Ogden wrote. But a warship, the *Hunter*, sat where they intended to cross. Another, the *Lizard*, was stationed nearby, so they aimed for a spot in between the two at Wolfe's Cove. Ogden traveled in Arnold's canoe, and they ran into the "*Hunter*'s boat rowing against the shore."[18] Arnold gave orders to "lay upon our paddles and let her pass,"[19] which it did without seeing the party.

Slowly they landed and formed on the Plains of Abraham. Twenty-seven men were in Arnold's first party to land. They sent the boats back across for the rest and surveyed the situation. "The scarcity of canoes made it very tedious getting over the men," he wrote. But the operation was complete by two o'clock the next morning. A party of sixteen was sent to take a house located nearby, and to their surprise, no one was inside.

In the darkness, a few heard voices from the river and, on inspection, found a boat rowing along the shore from one of the British ships to the other. They surprised them on a point of land, ordering the boat to "bring to." They answered "yes" but didn't and made a run for the current. The soldiers fired on them, and Ogden reported hearing the "shrieks of the wounded a long time."[20]

With the ranks now assembled on the Plains of Abraham, they marched up to Major Caldwell's house, where they found nobody around save a few servants, and took possession, along with two or three horses left behind. In the morning, Mathias Ogden and Major Bigelow surveyed the walls of the upper town with Mr. Halstead. Upon his return, Arnold delegated the job of posting the sentries based on his new knowledge of the structure of Quebec. Ogden did so. The first skirmish came quickly.

The ship at Wolfe's Cove fired upon the shore. "I observed the guard turning out," Ogden wrote. "I ran as fast as possible to know the reason and found the enemy was sallying out, and gave alarm."[21] They marched up to the walls, but the enemy retreated, taking with them one of the sentries they had captured. They hoped for an engagement on the plains right there, but all they got was a volley of cannon fire in which no one was hurt. They needed reinforcements, and fast, so Arnold sent an express to Montgomery requesting his immediate assistance. Storming the city would have to wait.

Chapter 8

ATTACK ON FORT QUEBEC

Quebec City sat on an escarpment at the river's edge. Above, the Plains of Abraham stretched west beyond the boundary of the Upper Town. The Lower Town consisted of dwellings on the waterfront district. Unfortunately, the troublesome tip from Eneas still bore sour fruit for Arnold, and the message carried in from Norridgewock informed them of the expedition. The reality of his mistake now slammed Arnold square in the face. The British were waiting and, even worse, expected them.

Brigadier General Richard Montgomery advanced from the west in an effort that started at Fort Ticonderoga. Montreal provided no resistance for him, since the small company of British soldiers had evacuated the city two days prior to the Americans' arrival. Sorel fell next, and they moved on, hoping to provide the same result on Quebec, only this time Arnold and company would meet them in the middle if all went as planned.

Once again, the logistics of the march came to bear upon him. The cartridges prepared back on the march in the wake of the Dead River flood now proved useless, so Arnold had to pull back and wait while ammunition and other supplies were secured. Unlike in the villages of the Chaudière Valley, the residents of Quebec were torn over their allegiances. Now it was necessary to choose either a siege or an immediate assault. Colonel Allan Maclean had entered the city and organized a resistance to the American effort only the day before.

"Mr. Glenney, a gentleman who came to us (and had left town this morning) confirmed the information of Col. Maclean's arrival, with 200 of his regiment and about 80 of the Eighth."[1] With this information in hand, they "lost all hopes of taking the town by storm," Ogden wrote.

Arnold tried for the improbable: he asked them to surrender. He sent Ogden carrying the letter outlining the horrors they should expect if the terms of the surrender were not met. Ogden took a drummer with him, as was the custom, and approached St. John's gate waving the flag. "I was saluted with a eighteen-pound shot from the wall," he wrote. "It struck very near and spattered us with the earth it threw up."[2] They retreated immediately.

Ogden pondered the response being for technical procedural reasons he called "out of season," and Arnold wasn't satisfied either, so they made a return performance the next day. The response was the same, only with a smaller cannon fired from a different part of the wall in order, Ogden surmised, to have a greater chance at accuracy. Ogden's account strangely ends here in mid-sentence. His prominence in the battle carried on though.

Arnold removed his troops to Point aux Trembles, some twenty-five miles to the west, and waited for Montgomery to back him up.

The army, still barefoot and dressed in rags, remained in need. All with shoemaking skills were employed in transforming some leather taken from Tory houses into serviceable footwear. In a memorandum sent to General Montgomery on November 20, Arnold compiled his needs in this regard: "600 pairs of coarse stockings, 500 yards of coarse woolen for breeches, 1,000 yards of flannel or baize for shirts, 300 milled caps, 300 pairs of mittens or gloves, 300 blankets, powder and ball, a barrel of rum, and a barrel of sugar 10."[3] At the same time, Arnold reported to Montgomery that his cash was nearly exhausted. So far his expenditures had amounted to about £392, sterling, and he thought that it would not be expedient to offer paper to the Canadians for the further purchases that he now required. Evidence exists that Arnold frequently used his own funds to make up the difference that Congress refused to recognize at this point in the young War for Independence.

To Arnold, his army came first, finances be damned. He dispatched Aaron Burr's cousin Captain Matthias Ogden "with a letter to Prince and Haywood, Merchants, asking that, if the captain had insufficient funds to cover his purchases, the goods be charged to Arnold's account."[4]

Montgomery left a garrison behind to hold Montreal and took three hundred men downriver to Arnold's camp at Point aux Trembles (Neuville), landing there on December 3. With him, "he brought supplies, including British clothing captured from the 7th and 26th British Regiments, to the relief of Arnold's haggard band."[5] With these bare bones supplies and troops, Montgomery settled on an assault, since a siege seemed unfeasible. Moreover, many of the malcontented troops' enlistments ran out at the fast-approaching end of the year. They prepared for an attack that began in a snowstorm in the early dawn of December 31.

At the encampment, things were far from ideal. The smallpox epidemic that had caused them to build a hospital on the Great Carrying Place now broke out at Point aux Trembles. "The smallpox is all around us, and there is great danger of its spreading in the army," wrote Caleb Haskell.[6] Furthermore, spies were being sent out from the city every day; both men and women were discovered and taken prisoner. Haskell was busy and on hand in the capture of a schooner full of provisions bound for Quebec.

On December 11, plying the British in the Upper Town from their fortifications in the Lower Town, Arnold used Jemima Warner as a decoy, sent to the gate of the citadel of Quebec. She was killed by a well-placed shot "from the city" for her trouble.[7] Likewise, Mrs. Grier was killed on April 18, 1776.[8] Warner and Grier had to have been among the first of their sex to die in battle for the American cause.

They fired cannons on the city, with subsequent return fire for the next several days. It got close enough to Arnold himself that he abandoned his headquarters for a safer location, and one man was killed on December 16. Arnold was determined to storm the city. And so the preparations continued in this manner until the day of reckoning arrived as the year 1775 ended.

The pre-dawn of 1776 came in cold and snowy. For three days prior, the troops had been ordered to be prepared to "storm the Town at the shortest notice."[9] Finally, at two o'clock in the morning, with ladders ready, the troops assembled for the assault. Thirty shells lobbed into the city through the blizzard provided cover. Montgomery assembled on the Plains of Abraham to the west, while Arnold commanded the two divisions from Cambridge. Major Brown, with a company of Boston troops, and Colonel Livingston, with a regiment of Canadians, were to mount a false attack on the walls to the south of the St. John's gate. At five o'clock in the morning, the three waves were to begin this three-pronged assault on Quebec City.[10]

Montgomery and a company of carpenters cut the pickets at Cape Diamond, and the general pulled them "down with his own hand" and entered with his aide-de-camp, M'Pherson, an engineer, Mr. Anthill and Captain Cheeseman and the carpenters. The troops didn't follow suit. Waiting for them was a charge of grapeshot from the cannons and small arms, killing the gallant general and the others. Silence followed.[11]

Meanwhile, Arnold sent an advance company of thirty men with ladders forward, followed by an artillery company, with Daniel Morgan and his company of riflemen traveling around the wharf on the ice if possible. Deep snow foiled Morgan on this route, and the artillery piece had to be abandoned in the drifts. Arnold and company were under constant fire while they stumbled around in the dark amid the buildings and wharfs, unable to return fire. Morgan, in frustration, attacked the battery, as others vaulted the walls with the ladders. It happened so fast that they quickly took the battery and captured the guard of thirty men. This was a good start by any reckoning; however, it was here that a musket ball found its way into Arnold's leg, leaving a lasting wound that plagued him for the rest of his days. He was removed back to the hospital immediately as Morgan secured the battery.

David Wooster, now in command, later wrote Schuyler, pleading for help:

> *To General Schuyler.*
> *Sir:—The enclosed letters from Colonel Arnold and Colonel Campbell will inform you of the unhappy fate of our brave and most amiable friend, General Montgomery, who, with his Aid-de-camp, Macpherson, Captain Cheeseman, and several other brave officers and men, gloriously fell in an unfortunate attack on Quebeck—unfortunate, indeed, for in addition to the loss we sustain in the death of the General, one of the bravest men of the age, the flower of the Army at Quebeck were either cut off or taken prisoners. I little expect, with the troops who remain, to be able to continue the siege; in short, our situation in this country is at present, and will be till we have relief from the Colonies, very critical and dangerous. We really have but very few men in the country, and many of those few not to be depended on, as we have too dearly proved…*
>
> *Something must be done, and that speedily, or I greatly fear that we are ruined.*
>
> *…I expected you were at Congress, and had prepared to send this melancholy news to General Washington, as well as to you; but the post arriving last night, I find that you were at Albany; therefore, shall take it to you. I most heartily condole with you, with General Montgomery's friends, and with the country, for so great a public loss.*
>
> *I have the honour to be, your most obedient and very humble servant, David Wooster.*[12]

But it was not to be. Montgomery's army retreated after witnessing his demise, so reinforcements were now nil. Nor would any be coming. With three times the numbers behind the wall of the Upper Town and in the houses, the Morgan-led company was surrounded by fire. To make matters worse, another company stationed at the north side of the river St. Charles laboring to join the main force was attacked through the palace gate and taken prisoner. In all, the fire lasted five hours. They held on until 10:00 a.m. before surrendering to British forces. The wounded included Arnold, Captain Hubbard, Captain Lamb, Lieutenant Steele, Lieutenant Tisdale and Brigade Major Mathias Ogden.[13]

Sabatis and Natanis were the only Indians to fight on the American side. Natanis was "wounded in the wrist"[14] in the effort, a sort of redemption for his previous treatment and disdain by his commander, Arnold. The prisoners were well cared for and housed in the seminary at the Jesuits College. Montgomery was given a good burial service, at which his honor and goodness of heart were proclaimed for all to hear. The Battle of Quebec was officially lost.

On August 18, 1776, the captives Simon Fobes, Reuben Johnson and John Pollack, who had been held on a British ship, arranged a berry-picking trip with their captors. Wearing castoff clothes, they managed to slip away, ford a stream over a rope bridge and gain passage on a ferry across the St. Lawrence, where they retraced the route back down the Kennebec and made their way home.[15] "We came upon human bones and hair scattered about on the ground promiscuously," he wrote. "It was doubtless the spot where some of our fellow soldiers perished the Fall before on their way to Quebec." As had been the case that fall, rains hampered them now, "raising the streams to make it difficult, and sometimes dangerous, crossing."[16]

Fobes arrived unexpectedly at his parents' house in Massachusetts at the end of September 1776. He was visibly changed, his face pockmarked and haggard. His mother thought he was a straggler looking for food as he sat in a chair in their kitchen until his younger sister pronounced proudly, "La, if there ain't Simon!" When this sank in, his mother was "well-nigh overcome and came near swooning."[17]

While the attempt against Canada was a failure, the expedition soon took on an epic proportion akin to Hannibal's crossing of the Alps and Xenophon and the ten thousand Greeks for which it deserves. Logistics, as Professor Huston concludes, was a crucial element,[18] especially in transportation and, to a lesser extent, hospitalization and evacuation. Arnold's later treachery subverted the due credit unduly, and for the Colburns, who were responsible for the logistics and planning, the black mark of failure and the skullduggery of Arnold stalked them until this very day. The enemy was at first nature, and Colburn, his boats, scouts and personal expertise helped see the army through to their goal. Arnold performed brilliantly, resupplying the dying forces just in time. Many of the oft-maligned bateaux went the distance. Huston concluded, "Yet in spite of all difficulties, and in spite of the tragic ending, Arnold's march to Quebec remains one of the most remarkable feats of its kind in American annals."[19]

The fleet and youthful Aaron Burr, always quick to look out for himself, raced through behind Arnold, sticking "close to glory" that would not come to him for quite some time, giving no thought of helping those mired behind him. Burr was more concerned with maintaining the affections of the Indian maiden Jacataqua, who had accompanied him since Fort Western, if this part of the folklore is true. But he went on to earn his captain's commission, carrying correspondence from Arnold to Sorel, so his personal strategy paid off.

Word of the failure came to Washington at Cambridge and was met with great disappointment. The Revolution had met its first great defeat. John Adams left General Washington and Cambridge for Philadelphia and his seat in the Continental Congress haunted by the possibility that we might fail in our fight for independence.[20] The feeling would continue in the coming years.

Far to the north, the Colburn brothers floated home in bateaux they had built with their own hands from somewhere near the headwaters of the Dead River and continued on with their lives. They must have been satisfied that they had done their best. That included fighting in the rest of the Revolutionary War to come. Signs of the army's passage were visible seventy years after the march, when lumbermen working in the area noticed that "paths cut through the forests" could be "distinctly traced." At "Chain Lake, fragments of boats" were found.[21]

Expedition Plaque at Eustis, Maine. *Author's collection.*

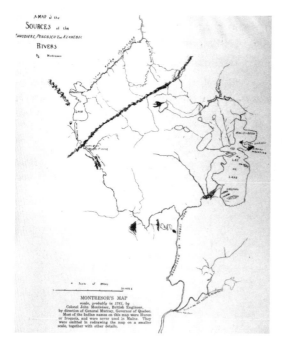

Montresor's map. *Courtesy of the Library of Congress.*

Washington's Headquarters, Cambridge, 1775. *Courtesy of the National Park Service.*

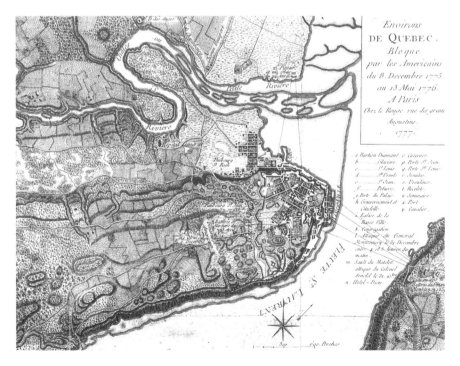

Attack on Quebec. *Courtesy of the Library of Congress.*

Arnold Pond. *Author's collection.*

Colburn House State Historic Site, 2011. *Author's collection.*

The parlor at Colburn House. *Author's collection.*

Major Colburn's wine closet. *Author's collection.*

Colonel Arnold. *Courtesy of the Library of Congress.*

King George III. *Courtesy of the Library of Congress.*

Pownalborough Courthouse, Dresden, Maine. *Author's collection.*

Arnold bedroom at Colburn House. *Author's collection.*

John Hancock, by John Singleton Copley. *Courtesy of the Library of Congress.*

Withstanding the Attack of Arnold's Men at the Second Barrier, by Sidney Adamson. *Courtesy of the Library of Congress.*

Fort Halifax. *Author's collection.*

Sarampus Falls, North Branch Dead River. *Author's collection.*

Working Against the Flood on Dead River, by Sidney Adamson. *Courtesy of the Library of Congress.*

Above, left: *Henry Dearborn,* by Gilbert Stuart. *Courtesy of the Library of Congress.*

Above, right: Daniel Morgan. *Courtesy of the Library of Congress.*

Above, left: Aaron Burr. *Courtesy of the Library of Congress.*

Above, right: Washington at Dorchester Heights, 1775. *Courtesy of the Library of Congress.*

On the last portage of the Great Carrying-Place, drawn by Denman Fink; half-tone plate engraved by H. Davidson. *Courtesy of the Library of Congress.*

Arnold's letter to Colburn, August 1775. *Courtesy of the National Archives Administration.*

Washington's orders to Colburn. *Courtesy of the National Archives Administration.*

Carrying the Bateaux at Skowhegan, by Sidney Adamson. *Courtesy of the Library of Congress.*

Above: Colburn to Washington.
Courtesy of the Library of Congress.

Left: Chaudière Map, 1760,
Height of Land. John Montresor.
Courtesy of Wikimedia Commons.

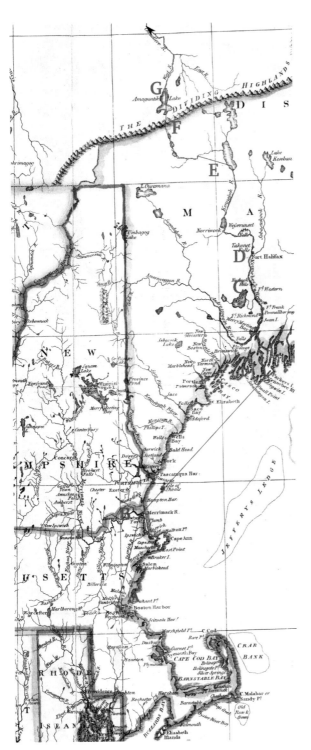

Arnold expedition route.
Courtesy of Wikimedia Commons.

Chapter 9

REVOLUTIONARY BROTHERS

D id Reuben Colburn, in the midst of his economic activities, march off to the war in the south? A Reuben Colburn enlisted in the Continental army in early 1781. "Receipt dated Dracut, March 22, 1781, for bounty paid said Colburn by the town of Dracut for enlisting into the Continental Army for the term of three years, agreeable to resolve of Dec. 2, 1780."[1] Is this the same Reuben Colburn? No, it was a younger cousin.

It is unlikely that Major Colburn, who would have been forty-one at the time with seven kids, returned to Dracut, the birthplace of his father, Jeremiah, and the rest of his family, to enlist and therefore obtain the bounty offered by Dracut. This Reuben Colburn had been a private in the Continental army on and off since 1777. He would have been a second cousin born in 1761, the year when the Jeremiah Colburn family moved to Maine. Major Reuben Colburn was born in 1740. Major Reuben Colburn served in "Private Service," according to the Daughters of the American Revolution records. His brothers were commissioned for short periods, as was common at the time. They were militia members, as were many American Patriots. No doubt, Major Colburn was enraged by the treason of General Arnold and felt strongly in service to the American cause, which was very shaky at this point, for Arnold, as anyone who had served under him knew, was a capable and courageous leader. That is what made his defection so unthinkable. But Colburn never became a commanding general. The Continental army was full with them competing for credit, as Arnold found out the hard way. Throughout his life, Major Reuben

Colburn served as a commander in a militia cavalry based in Pittston. He was a striking figure, no doubt, on horseback with long sword in scabbard and a three-cornered hat. Regardless of opinion, Colburn and Arnold are married, for better or worse, in history forever.

The story of his older brother Jeremiah Jr. and his sons is of a different nature. Jeremiah was willed much of the land in Pittston by his father, Jeremiah Sr., in 1765, along with the 250 acres willed to Reuben on which his house now stands. For reasons that are hard to understand, Jeremiah Jr., four years older than Reuben, chose to move on to the uncharted Indian country of the central Penobscot River, some eighty miles to the east of the Kennebec. We can only speculate as to why he chose to leave the rest of his family and explore other regions, but it was at the very least a courageous act for a man with two young children to care for. With his two young sons, Jeremiah and William, the eldest of the Colburn brothers arrived in the location of present-day Orono on Stillwater Island sometime in 1766 with a partner from Dunstable, Mr. Ayres. The region was entirely in the hands of the Penobscot tribe, to which the new immigrants announced their intentions to clear land, build sawmills and start a lumbering endeavor.

The Penobscot tribe, having no previous bad experiences with the colonists, gave them their permission to build on their land. They built a house and mill on the island and proceeded with the operation as planned. The Colburns continued the family tradition of cooperation with their Indian neighbors—or landlords, as it were—contrary to current historical perspective that only concentrates on the opposite, adversarial relationships in our country's origins. For their efforts in business and diplomacy, they prospered for the next nine years until the British arrived to commandeer the area's resources for their efforts to squelch the colonial uprising now in progress. They had started the first "Great Northern" lumber business still found in the region today in the form of the paper industry of the same name, the largest private landowner in the East. Again, like his brother Reuben in the shipping business, a Colburn was first.

While hard at work on the property in 1775—exactly when is unknown, but perhaps after the failed Arnold expedition, despite the great effort engineered by his brother Reuben—British soldiers marched onto Jeremiah's land with the intention to confiscate it for their cause. Mr. Ayres, not being the "revolutionary" type, agreed to the terms immediately, perhaps with self-preservation as a motivating factor, or perhaps a yellow streak. Nevertheless, Jeremiah Colburn Jr. would have no part of it and announced they "would rather have tyrants' chains about their necks and look out prison windows, than be false to their country."[2] To Jeremiah Jr. and his teenage sons, England was not their country. America was. And they were loyal to it.

What the British commander said is easy to speculate. They were given time to obey or else. When left to their own devices, the Colburns buried their belongings "in a dry place" and in the dead of night left for Pittston, with plans to return once the oppressors were put in their proper place, however long and with whatever effort was required for the job. Some days later, they arrived at Jeremiah's parents' house next to Reuben's and planned the immediate future. It is a family meeting that one today would love to have been in on. Fierce patriotism was the Colburn family policy; with the sting of the failure of the Arnold expedition, and now this insult, inaction was not an option.

The Colburn Militia was on guard, but local involvement was not enough for the elder Colburn, who soon left for Camden to join the Continental army. Thus, in late 1775, the three Colburns—Jeremiah Jr., age thirty-nine; Jeremiah III, seventeen; and William, at just fifteen— entered the federal service in defense of their country against the most powerful empire the world had ever known. They did it without a thought to their own safety, only to the cause at hand.

Jeremiah Jr. was given a lieutenant's commission in Captain Foster's company and placed in charge of the arsenal at Camden. His son and namesake became a fifer in Captain Walker's company. William was with him. This arrangement worked well until the British captured the three Patriots while they were attempting to defend the arsenal. The boys escaped in the night, vowing to free their father. Why Jeremiah did not join them is unclear. He remained a prisoner for the rest of the war. The boys returned to their company and continued to serve. Legend has it that the musket carried by William that night in Camden remained in the family for many years and still may somewhere.

After the war, the united family returned to Orono but found their home and buildings gone. The belongings buried there in 1775 were still intact. They rebuilt and took up where they had left off in the lumber business. Eventually, Jeremiah sold much of his land to John Marsh Jr., his son-in-law, who later would will it to the State of Maine for the location of the new University of Maine.[3] Jeremiah Colburn Jr. died in 1811 at the home of William Colburn that still stands on Bennoch

Road in Orono, where he spent his later years in the care of his youngest son, one of the last living Revolutionary soldiers left when he died in 1847. His elder brother Jeremiah III died in Orono in 1786 of unknown causes. William's portrait still adorns the stairwell his father built.

Chapter 10

MAINE OPERATIONS

L ife had to go on as always despite the setbacks encountered. Reuben Colburn concentrated on his lumber and shipbuilding operations even as the Revolution raged on in the south and west.

In 1778, Colburn created a company called Reuben Colburn and Associates, which became involved in the exploration of a northern route across New England. He competed with a collection of early explorers to the Sandy River country in western Maine to open up the territory to settlement. At the request of John Hancock, Colburn officially became engaged in the details of the survey and settlement of what would become the present-day city of Farmington, Maine. The full length of the route through to the Connecticut River was abandoned.[1]

The first party consisted of Stephen Titcomb, Robert Gower, James Henry, Robert Alexander and James Macdonnell. Their guide was Thomas Wilson, who had previously explored the region as a hunter. In 1776, the party came up from Topsham to Hallowell in canoes. Hallowell at this time consisted of four or five houses and some warehouses for storing fish. Over a "bad road" with few settlers, they made their way out to Winthrop on a west-northwest compass bearing through today's Mount Vernon and Vienna, striking the Sandy River at New Sharon Falls. From there, they followed the river up to Farmington Falls, where Reuben Colburn would later locate the first mills. Farther upstream, they staked out the boundaries where they wanted to carve their farms by stripping the bark from some basswood trees. Having completed this task, they returned to Topsham to obtain tools and supplies, hoping to return in two weeks to commence clearing the land.

The official proclamation came from Boston three years later assigning Colburn the official survey duties. By a memorandum signed in Boston on October 4, 1779, by James Bowdoin, Daniel Jeffers, James Hewing and John Hancock, and from an alteration annexed, dated at Boston, March 3, 1780, signed by Henry Allen, proprietor's clerk, the following arrangement was made with the Committee of the Proprietors of the Kennebec Purchase by Reuben Colburn and his Associates, viz:

> *That the Associates should cause a survey to be taken of all that tract of land west of Kennebec River and north of the southerly line of Settler's Lot No. 70, in the town of Vassalborough, now Sidney, and south of the mouth of Sandy River, and extending westerly fifteen miles: viz[2]*

While the first party was hopeful to settle the region, it took Reuben Colburn to make the official survey a reality. There was money to be made, and he intended to be first. And he was.

It appears that the survey was completed and the returns made, agreeably to directions, in June 1780 by Joseph North, Esq. But as it was considered somewhat doubtful whether the town would fall within the limits of the Plymouth Claim, no further measures were taken to obtain a title to the lands until after the Revolutionary War, when the boundaries were settled between the state and the Plymouth Company.[3]

The original title of his company had been the Proprietors of a Township on Sandy River until the change to Reuben Colburn and Associates took place on December 17, 1777, two years after the Arnold expedition. Members included in the company were Dummer Sewall, Francis Tufts and Samuel Butterfield. Colburn built the first mills, as evidenced in the historical record. The road was surveyed during the first winter and the question of proprietorship wrestled with. The western part of the road traveled a river-notch path into the part of the valley where the towns of Byron and Andover now sit.

Passing through the valley, Colburn and his party came across a pond where they found a pile of rusted traps at the base of a tree in which was carved "Thos. Webb." Thus, they named the lake for this bold trapper: Webb Lake. The name remains to this day.

> *In was agreed by the Associates, July 4 1780, that Reuben Colburn and Stephen Pullen should build the mills at Sandy River, upon their giving bonds that it should be done by the first of August, 1781, and that they*

should be kept in repair seven years. The sawmill was first put in operation in Nov 1781, and the gristmill in the following August.[4]

It is unclear just how much hand labor Colburn did himself, as he was a businessman concerned with setting up the operation and hiring the workers with the skills needed, as he had in his shipyard. It could be safely said that he was no stranger to hard labor of any kind. A flood in 1785 damaged the mills severely, on account of the dam being defective, and the new settlers "suffered greatly for want of facilities for procuring grinding, and were compelled to go to Winthrop to mill, a part of the time, for some years, and frequently with hand sleds. To remedy this hardship many of them prepared mortars with a spring-pole to raise the pestle, by the help of which they made tolerable meal."[5]

While on the ground in these efforts, Reuben Colburn was also in the midst of the political and legal efforts as well. The man is omnipresent in this era, both as a local and national leader and a state lawmaker. The account of the Massachusetts General Court on which he served cemented the Sandy River operation.

Commonwealth of Massachusetts
In Senate, February 4th, 1790
...Reuben Colburn and his Associates, should hold all the lots in said township marked with the letter S, in the said plan returned, a duplicate whereof accompanies this Resolve...
Sent down for concurrence. Thomas Daws, President Pro Tem
In the House of Representatives, February 4th, 1790.
Read and concurred David Cobb, Speaker[6]

That settled the legal situation. Colburn and others received several lots on which to settle and build their enterprises. While constructing and running the first mills, as with his mills in Skowhegan, Reuben had no need or desire to settle there. That was left to others. He remained at the home in Pittston and concentrated on his first love and endeavor—shipbuilding. The lands he collected in those early days in Maine passed through the hands of the family almost without trace. Descendants own almost none of it now, with the exception of the family of my great-grandfather Nelson Colburn (built by Oliver prior to 1788), who until recently still lived in the house on Route 27 between Pittston and Dresden on a fraction of the land willed to Oliver by Jeremiah Sr. Reuben's house and remaining parcel of land belongs to the

State of Maine. It is the Colburn House State Historic Site, and the result of decades-long restoration efforts is now finally coming to fruition.

Later, statehood was a goal of Major Colburn when almost no one dared to separate from Massachusetts. He was a delegate to the Falmouth Convention in 1786[7] that weighed this very issue. This was the first time a body met to decide the fate of the territory of Maine concerning separation. Colburn voted in the affirmative, but at this time, the motion failed. Not until 1820, two years after his death, did the citizenry decide he had been right.

First in 1786, and again in 1796, Colburn took time away from his family and business concerns to serve as a representative to the Massachusetts General Court in Boston, requiring him to reside there while in session. Exactly where is not known, as is the case with many of the details of my great-grandfather's life, but with Governor Hancock as a close friend it can be safely assumed that Reuben had suitable accommodations in Boston.[8] It was here that Colburn cast a vote in the affirmative to ratify the U.S. Constitution for Massachusetts before the Congress finalized the historic bill on September 17, 1787. There aren't many who can make that claim.

During this time, he continued his close friendship with John Hancock, then the governor, formerly the president of the Congress. Hancock was a frequent visitor to the mansion when in Pittston, and Colburn housed an unruly, wayward nephew of Hancock's in an effort to set the young man on a straight and narrow path that the hard work of country life could instill. Reuben's dealings with Hancock included the selling of lumber, as one of his only surviving letters states:

> *To his Excellency John Hancock in Boston, Pittston, July 28, 1787*
> *Dear Sir,*
> *I have shipped fourteen sticks of fine timber, agreeable to your directions on board of William Porter—marked J.H. Sir, I have not collected one bit of lumber of Col. Worth; he has been in Boston sometime. As soon as he returns I shall endeavor to collect the other lumber and send it to you.*
>
> *I had agreed with Adam Gardner for your lumber, but his sudden death disappointed me. I am sorry it has not been in my power to send you your lumber. Mr. Harry Quincy has got him a cleaver house and moved into it with his family, and has got to work on the lot. He will do well.*
>
> *From your humble servant,*
> *Reuben Colburn*[9]

After the war, Reuben continued building ships, contributing to the national shipping heritage and promoting the American ideal. As one of the first American shipbuilders north of Bath,[10] along with his partner Thomas Agry, Colburn and his son David built schooners at the house and shipyard that exceeded one hundred feet in length and sailed the world under the American flag, engaged in trade and the War of 1812. Examples of these vessels built by these Pittston builders are as follows: *Criterion*, 1807; *Caroline*, 1807; *Emeline*, 1810; and, with Agry, *Dolphin*, 1784, and *Phenix*, 1788. These represent excellent examples of their contributions to American shipping history.[11] Ships built at the site by Colburn and Agry brought needed supplies from all over the world to the growing colonies, hence promoting American economic strength and security when the country was in its infancy and needed it the most.[12]

"At Cobbosseecontee [Gardiner] there is a considerable of shipbuilding going on, and a double sawmill and gristmill which employ thirty or forty hands." Covered in the statement were "Reuben Colburn and Thomas Agry who were said to have been building vessels as early as 1763 near the present town of Pittston."[13] The demand for shipbuilding locations and a new supply of timber that was readily available led to the spread north of this critical industry. The great era of shipbuilding on the Kennebec began in 1783.[14]

Congress's denial of payment for the bateaux caused Reuben and his family great financial hardship at a critical time in American history. He and other New England shipbuilders and traders were greatly hampered by the embargo on trade with Britain and France in the years prior to and during the War of 1812. Colburn had previously taken a contract to build a large ship for Peter Bryson of Wiscasset, and this vessel, partially constructed, was left to decay on the stocks in the yard below the house. Reuben was financially ruined. Debt was a disgrace in those days, and furniture was taken away by citizens to help cover the debts. His son David, a shipwright who built many large vessels in his father's shipyard in later years, came to his rescue and saved the family's reputation.[15]

"Sizable vessels—considering the type or rig and the times—were built at Pittston in almost every year. Building was suspended in 1813 and 1814 because of the war with Britain, but was resumed in 1815 with vigor."[16] Toward the end of Reuben Colburn's life, with David's help, the shipyard was recovering, but it would die off by the end of the 1830s, largely due to the implementation of the steam engine and a revival of British dominance at sea. A limited number of ships were built at

Pittston until the 1850s, when the wooden sailing ships of Colburn's era finally came to an end for good.

The shipping legacy of the Kennebec River pioneers cannot be ignored. Their industriousness, sheer ingenuity and unbridled courage sent them around the world in search of adventure and prosperity from the fruits of Maine. They returned with a love of Greek Revival architecture, exotic furniture and art from Constantinople and a host of treasures from distant lands beyond local imagination. Their floating homes housed their wives and children, who got an education far beyond anything to be found in books. Captain Reuben Colburn, Major Colburn's grandson, and David Lawrence, an in-law, were exactly this kind of men. Drowning at sea was always a risk (Lawrence was lost in such a way, leaving wife, Elizabeth, bereft at Colburn House), but that did not deter them from their quest to learn about the world as a whole. The homespun skills necessary for this type of task are hard to find, but they can be found in abundance in Pittston. They brought Maine to the world and the world to Maine.

Chapter 11

THE CLAIM

As Jefferson emerged the victor in the election of 1800, Colburn's claim for the bateaux still languished in the backrooms of power in the new capital of Washington City. England, however, was still not content to work with us. The embargo of President Thomas Jefferson, in his second term and later during the War of 1812 under his successor, James Madison, was disastrous for Colburn and his neighbors. It was at this time that he would have been believed to have abdicated his support of Jefferson, as many in New England did, even to the point of secessionist talk, but in Pittston, they voted against petitioning Jefferson to remove the embargo in 1808 and affirmed their support of him, his policies and his administration.[1] This Republican support continued for Madison and Monroe. After the war, Colburn's claim for payment for the bateaux came into full swing as his own life waned. In New England, unlike Virginia, debt was considered a crime and punishable by prison, as many found out. With his living destroyed, Colburn did what everyone did when their finances turned sour: he tried to collect old debts owed him. In Colburn's case, this led straight to George Washington. The new government that he supported with vigor, and with his own funds, now claimed it had never heard of his claim and had lost the evidence of his expenditures he provided at the time of his original submission.

Enter presidential ally and Secretary of the Treasury Alexander Hamilton and his brilliant work in this regard. During the Revolution, the U.S. government ran up a debt of $50 million acquired from its wealthiest citizens, and many of its not-so-wealthy citizenry, by selling them bonds to be paid back later with interest. With no way to pay back this debt, Hamilton proposed the selling of yet another set of thirty-year bonds at 6 percent interest to foreign speculators confident in the success of the new country. But his intentions were scurrilous, as he deliberately conspired to default on the citizens at the benefit of "foreign" speculators. This was unprecedented financial manipulation by an opportunist of great talent and position. James Madison pointed this out, with good reason and credit to his character. He proposed a bill addressing this discrimination between the two classes of bondholders, but the ever-clever Hamilton argued that "the logistics of tracking down and sorting out competing claims were prohibitively difficult and would discourage nervous foreign investors." The bill was defeated thirty-six to thirteen.[2] To no one's surprise, Jefferson, Madison and the Republicans saw this as an unprecedented assault on ordinary Americans in favor of wealthy "patrician" interests and a return to monarchy. The practice continued.

It was said that Jefferson set up a dinner meeting where he offered a proposal for accepting the Hamiltonian plan in exchange for building the new capital in Virginia. Regardless of when and where, the deal was accepted, and the capital was located where it is today. Hamilton wielded his powers at Treasury during the Washington administration and, in the view of many, started on the road to his demise, but not before his policies ruined, or attempted to ruin, faithful Patriots. Reuben Colburn wandered into this financial morass in the 1790s. Little did he know of this policy that any claim was deemed fraudulent by definition. There is reference to an "Act of Limitation" on Revolutionary claims in 1792–93 while Hamilton was in office, passed in hope of preventing payments. No claimant in the ensuing years appears to have been deterred, and in 1860, HR 686 was introduced to repeal this bill.[3]

But the process could be long and frustrating, more often than not failing, as this claim illustrates. Many of these private claims were submitted repeatedly to successive Congresses, and the process often stretched on long after the life of the original claimant. "The memorial of L. Madison Day, (49A-H5.1), gives voice to the frustrations of recovering damages from the government: 'This claim has been before Congress for some time, and has been many times favorably reported upon, four times in the House and five times in the Senate, and was passed by the Senate during the forty-seventh Congress, but was not reached for consideration in the House.'"[4]

The £26 recorded in Washington's logbook were held against a bill of £526, and the balance was never paid. Colburn, with the help of his congressional representatives, started a campaign that lasted fifty years. They filed the claim against the government with the State of Massachusetts within the proper time frame. Unfortunately, years passed without any action. It isn't known when or if the commissioner submitted Colburn's records to the Committee on Revolutionary Claims in Congress. In the *Journals of Congress*, the first report of a follow-up appeared in January 1796. Henry Dearborn, a captain in the Continental army on the march to Quebec, later a general and then a congressman from Massachusetts, presented Colburn's case and got a stay to provide time to recollect the information. By a vote of forty-one to thirty-eight, it was granted, and the battle ensued. I found all sixty-two pages of the Reuben Colburn Papers in the National Archives. They are still the property of Congress and included the letters from Arnold and Washington. The papers in this original recollection date to 1796, submitted as John Adams took office. They passed the case around like a hot hearthstone from that point on.

Colburn became one of the first government contractors to actually lose money on a contract, when today these contractors rip off the taxpayers by the millions on a daily basis. How times change. It was also a case of "defeat is an orphan, and success has many fathers." The mission to capture Quebec in 1775 failed, and Arnold by this time had become the symbol of treason. It was not a good thing to bring up in a claim for past debts, but inevitable. As the history books indicated, the bateaux leaked. With interest, £500-plus would add up to serious money, even in 1856.

"Colburn added paddles, oars, setting poles, and pikes to his bills as separate items. He apparently was never paid in full," wrote James Huston.

Washington had made payments of 117 for earlier services, and Arnold paid about 100 Pounds for the bateaux, but for these and other items the Continental Congress still owed, according to Colburn, about 368 Pounds...

In 1818, General Henry Dearborn, who served as a captain on Arnold's expedition, and later became Secretary of War, then General in Chief of the Army [and, like Reuben Colburn, moderator of Pittston], *testified to Congress to the justice of a claim on this account which Colburn made at that time. Final action on Colburn's claim did not come until March 1824, when Congress refused to approve payment largely on the ground that the lapse of so much time, and the loss of public records, made the justice of the claim doubtful!*[5]

It was common for the young government to commandeer the resources of its loyal citizen Patriots who were better off, and the record indicates that many weren't paid back after the conflict was resolved in our favor.

The Washington administration, considered Federalist, was the first to adopt this policy. Nathaniel Tracy, the shipping magnate of Newburyport who provided the eleven transports ships for the march to Quebec, was also not paid for his effort as Washington promised. "Loss or damage," wrote Washington in August 1775, "to be compensated by the public according to an estimation to be made before said vefsels proceed in the above service."[6] Tracy loaned the government great sums of money and financed many privateer vessels that were captured, and Congress never authorized repayment of the loans.[7] Though richer to begin with than Colburn, Tracy was ruined in much the same way for his great contribution. It was a trend.

This writer hasn't been able to locate the receipts for the rest of this money claimed to have been paid to Colburn and remains skeptical of its validity. Why hadn't Washington, by all accounts a stickler for details, kept a receipt of the £368, or £440 plus the £100 from Arnold, as he did with the £26 that he had records for? Did he get lax as the amount paid increased? It doesn't seem as though he would. Arnold was known to have paid for expenses out of his own pocket, so it is easy to imagine him giving Colburn the £100 at the shipyard, but why no record of this payment? Nonetheless, £440 is a significant personal expense spent by Colburn on the operation out of his pocket.

Justin Smith found Colburn's final bill in the Archives of Congress in 1902. The bill covers travel expenses to Quebec for Colburn and paying for repair supplies, a birch canoe, his guides (Isaac Hull, Dennis and Nehemiah Getchell and an Indian guide) "@ 4 days for a total of £445: 1: 7. 1786—July 3rd—errors, except, Reuben Colburn."[8]

Colburn swore in this statement in front of Judge EDM J.P. Quincy on the above date. The controversy simply would not go away. It is evident that bills incurred during the Revolution by the citizenry were meant to be sacrifices to the cause by the new ruling body in Congress. During this time, the 1780s, the Federalist Party, led by Alexander Hamilton and John Adams to a lesser degree, did battle with the Republicans led by Thomas Jefferson. The nation was concerned with getting on its feet and avoiding a war with France, which we did with the leadership of Adams. The politics of George Washington were more ambiguous, but he leaned toward Federalist. The idea of a semi-royal immune executive branch didn't lend itself to the struggle of the little man, and today it still holds true.

Colburn's struggle to be paid money owed him from 1775 was in many ways too small a detail for the leadership to concern themselves with by the time he realized that the bills had been lost by the federal representative from Massachusetts charged with the duty of processing the request to the Treasury Department. Lacking receipts from Arnold, Hamilton's treasury denied the claim on this bureaucratic technicality, and Colburn, like many others, went to Congress for justice.

These claims were numerous to the point that the committee of claims could almost predict with certainty that many were fraudulent and therefore were dismissed, justly so. The Colburn case seems to test their accuracy by dismissing such a prominent case with substantial evidence of validity and support by prominent citizens and representatives of Congress itself. It seems blatantly obvious what they were up to. All claims were to be dismissed regardless of merit, as per Hamiltonian decree that eventually became law just in time to quell Colburn for good. Until then, the method was to keep postponing the thing forever. Colburn went through hell for this mission and wasn't about to give up. To him, business was business.

Congress would not budge. In the early days of bureaucratic bungling, Colburn's paperwork submitted in Boston never made it to the capital. All the while, he must have thought the wheels just moved slowly but moved in his favor nonetheless. In reality, those in charge weren't even aware of the matter. What brought this to Colburn's attention isn't known in detail, but the lack of money is obvious. He must have been livid when he confronted the commissary of Massachusetts on the matter and learned his files had been lost. Colburn moved fast to file a stay in Congress with the committee on claims in hope of re-gathering the records and submitting them in person. It was 1786, eleven years after the march, while he served in the Massachusetts House of Representatives for the first time.

Congress was busy passing and ratifying the Constitution, no small matter in history. Details of this nature were easy to push aside. However, Colburn was successful in getting them to reconsider the case, beginning a long series of postponements by the committee requiring constant attention and resubmitting by Massachusetts and Maine representatives in Congress on Colburn's behalf. Each time it was as if the body had never heard of the claim, and they always referred it back for further study. Colburn never relented. Congress never ceased to be dense.

Another bill accounts for £522 total for the two hundred bateaux, including paddles and setting poles, feeding the carpenters, the initial scouting operation and Colburn's trips to Cambridge. These last two categories differ from the ones submitted by Henry Dearborn in his December 9 testimony to Congress on Colburn's behalf (£27: 15 shillings: 3 pence and £152: 10: 6, respectively). The differences are small, but in all scenarios, the deficit owed Colburn is large. Colburn received £26 pounds from Washington and £35 pounds, 16 shillings for transporting the Indian chiefs to Watertown on August 15 as an allowance for travel expenses. The next order of business is the testimony of Arnold to Washington that he paid Colburn £100 pounds cash for the extra twenty bateaux. That would bring his paid total to £161, 16 shillings. At any rate, there is no receipt for the so-called £100 payment by Arnold that this author or any other could find. Nor does Washington account for it. It is certain they would have recorded it based on the other entries and receipts.

However, as was later documented, Arnold frequently paid for supplies and services out of his own pocket. In Quebec, he bought clothing for frozen troops, hoping for reimbursement from Washington later. It can't be overemphasized that this war was run on a shoestring budget, but this operation weighed more heavily on Colburn than normal even in this sad state of affairs.

Colburn supplied the workforce from his local crew that he and partner Thomas Agry employed with regularity. The detail of his charges is complete in all areas. The last batch of bateaux, twenty in number, that Arnold ordered after his arrival were given to Agry to fill while Colburn saw to other matters. His receipt:

> *Gardinerstown, Sept. the 30th 1775*
> *Then recd of Capt. Reuben Colburn Twelve Pounds lawful money it being in full for the building of the Last Twenty Battoes. I say recd by me.*
> *Thomas Agry*[9]

Thusly, Arnold's receipt only mentions product delivered sans payment of any amount:

> *Received Kenebeck Sept. 1775 of Mr. Reuben Colburn,*
> *Two Hundred & Twenty Batteau's for the Publick Service.*
> *Bt. Arnold*[10]

Arnold's use of "Mr.," as Justin Smith notes, clearly shows that Colburn's military titles were for service in the militia, not a commission in the Continental army. His service designation is "PS" for private service in the registry of the DAR.[11] Further receipts cement the trend that Colburn kept track of every detail when it came to monetary matters.

> *Gardinerstown Sept. 15th 1775 Recd of Capt. Ruben Colburn the full sum of Teen pound 14 and Eight pence Lawful Money for fifty four days work at ye Battoes.*
> *L 10. 14. 8*
> *Nathaniel Stevens*[12]

The next bill is, on the surface, confusing. These charges for fifty-seven days for these men doesn't fit the time frame of the operation. Smith hypothesized they might represent four crews under their supervision, and this seems appropriate. He also accuses Colburn of padding the bill in this way that doesn't appear to stand much scrutiny. The labor bill is a small part of the charges for the total order. Washington's price of "40 shillings a piece" with poles and oars accounts for the deficit denied Colburn on the account, not inflated labor charges, as implied in the quip by Smith. "Possibly we may see here a hint of the method used by Colburn to execute so large a contract," Smith wrote. The number would refer to man hours, not actual number of days worked.

> *Gardinerstown Sept. 15th 1775*
> *Recd of Capt. Ruben Colburn the full sum of Nine pound Six & Eight pence Lawful Money for 57 days Work done at Building Battoes.*
> *Edward Savage*
> *Joseph Savage*
> *Daniel Hilton*
> *Michall Rierdan*[13]

Colburn's impassioned plea to Congress in 1799 illustrates the erudition and dignity with which he served his young country and implored the government to honor his claim after the massive bungling by those who had involved themselves in the case to date. It will continue as a source of pride for family members today. Colburn testifies that he asked Washington about the balance in the winter of 1776, right after the failed mission occurred—not the first incidence of bad timing in the story.

Washington replied that he needed to have the receipts from Arnold to grant the final payment to Colburn. Washington mentions at this time the "great service" Colburn provided to the expedition and his country. However,

Washington never received the accounts from Arnold, and Colburn submitted everything to the commissioner in New York for proper review. They remained there long after the death of that representative, and nothing was done until Colburn discovered the foul-up and wrote this testimony:

To the Honorable the Senate and the House of Representatives of the Congress of the United States of America…

Your petitioner begs leave respectively to state that in the year 1775 he was employed by proper authority in conveying the American troops up Kennebeck river on their expedition to Quebec. In doing which great expenses devolved upon him as will appear by his accounts, & other documents now on your honors files.__ That in the winter after said services were done, your petitioner applied to General Washington for an adjustment to his accounts; he replied he had not received from Genl. Arnold, the bills, or certificates of the expenses on the expedition, therefore could not comply with your petitioner's request. At the same time, the General admitted your petitioner had done much in aiding that expedition.__ Some time afterward, your petitioner's accounts were committed to the proper officer at Boston for allowance, as since appears they were served as yours to the commissioner at New York who soon afterward died.__ There it seems they remained about six years without anything being done thereon or your petitioners knowing where they were. In the meantime your petitioner applied to Congess—the accounts were sought for at the office at Philadelphia, but in vain.__ After a long space of time spent in inquiry those papers were found at New York, as above stated.__ Hence the failure in not having the business brought before Congess at a much earlier period.__ The proof thereof, the Hon. George Thatcher and Henry Dearborn Esquires, then representatives can testify. Your petitioner, therefore humbly conveys he is not accusable of negligence in the case.__ But the delay was occasfioned as he has been informed, by mislaying his papers in a departmental office of the government…Much of the time and vigor of your petitioner's life—and much of his property were expended in the service of his country—in consequence thereof; and through the great delays & embarasfments attendant on producing his original demands before Congess, he in an advanced age, is reduced to indignant circumstances; from which the justice of government may extricate him and enable him to spend the remainder of life free from the straits of pennilessness—With sentiments of great respect; and as in duty bound, will ever pray.[14]

Reuben Colburn
Pittston, Nov.—1799

It was a noble address, a valiant effort of a Patriot to get his due justice. As the administration of John Adams and the life of George Washington ended, the turn of the century brought a new cast of characters, but the result was the same. Allies from the expedition came to his aid, and one, General Henry Dearborn, his good friend and Pittston resident, was about to ascend to the position of secretary of war after the contentious election of 1800 in the new administration of Thomas Jefferson. One would think, at least in today's political world, that those kinds of connections would get even a dishonest, illegitimate government contractor funds to which he claimed a right; but not here. The scourge of the legacy of Arnold, then near death in exile in London, held firm to Colburn's effort. All connected to Arnold were shunned.

In Norwich, Connecticut, the home of Arnold's birth was flattened as the symbol of disgrace, likewise later his New Haven home, lest anyone try to commemorate him and his "dark act." The traitor image blanketed all associated with the once-great Patriot commander. For Reuben Colburn, his task was quite an obstacle, but the effort continued, nevertheless, with the papers and testimonies submitted in 1796, including those of Dearborn and Samuel Berry, the initial scout for the expedition:

> *Although he has made diligent search for several years could not find them until within a few days, by which means the claim of your memorialist is now by the auditor of the Treasury convinced as being banned by the limitation act, and consequently cannot be settled at the treasury, your memorialist is therefore under the necessity of applying to Congrefs for a settlement of his demand having no doubt but that ample justice will be done him.*
>
> Henry Dearborn
> On behalf of Reuben Colburn
> February 2nd, 1795

Samuel Berry hailed from Bath and settled in the West Gardiner area on Plaisted Hill, where he cut timber and built a farm on his eight-acre homestead. He was tall, had a long, black beard and dressed in buckskins and a coonskin cap. A noted trapper and woodsman, Berry, it was said, "could cover more ground on snowshoes with his great stride than any man in the territory; seven feet between strides when measured."[15]

Colburn and company made most of the way to Canada, according to Berry:

The defendant went with Col. Arnold as far as the head of the Chaudière River,___I know that said Colburn set out from Fort Western three days before I did, and he returned two days before I did, and I was forty two days from the time I left Fort Western until I returned.[16]
Samuell Berry

Colburn's bills account for £140 or £150 pounds credited to the U.S. government. It seems likely, even sans receipt from Arnold for the extra twenty bateaux, that this is what the bulk of this credit can be attributed to. That ultimately leaves the outstanding balance of £440 pounds, more or less within a few pounds, still owed Colburn. There is no record that supports the observation of Professor James A. Huston that Colburn had been paid £117 by Washington, plus £100 by Arnold. Only one can be accounted for, not both. The evidence is not there, and as I've noted, the receipt from Arnold has never been found. Only in Colburn's credit to the government is a £100 amount recorded. Therefore, the £440 balance is correct.

Congress remained adamant. In 1796, as John Adams took office, the first negative decision was rendered: "Mr. Dearborn urged that the petitioner had done everything in his power to lodge his claim within the time limited by law. He [Dearborn] asked a further postponement for the sake of getting information."[17] But Mr. Harper declared that it was the fault of Colburn, whose own "negligence" created the mishap, and he was ready to decide the question right then. The vote in favor of a deferment went to Colburn, forty-one to thirty-eight.

This had to be the most legitimate and prominent of all the Revolutionary claims of the time. Clearly, many were frivolous and fraudulent attempts to get money from the government, but this was truly a case of taking advantage of a legitimate contractor who gave his all for an operation to create America from the ground up. Denying the Colburn claim as an illegitimate scheme on Colburn's part after the extensive records were misplaced and ignored for years is an insult to his patriotism. Which is why in 1799, prompted by the financial pressures felt by many of his peers, Colburn rode down a snowy trail all the way to Mount Vernon to see Washington and discuss the matter man to man. If it happened, it is a story of legendary proportions.[18] It is easy to imagine, but I have no confirmation that it is true. It sounds like something Reuben would do. Never doubt the voracity of a Mainer when it comes to money.

"Sir, I'm very sorry, but the president is dead," said the doorman while a shocked Colburn doffed his hat on the porch in respect. Imagine his disappointment and grief to learn that the ex-president he worked for, and who held Reuben's last hope of payment, had died just the night before.[19] Colburn thus joined in the crestfallen atmosphere that engulfed Mount Vernon. It was a stroke of incredibly bad luck. That Washington died after a short ride around his plantation from a streptococcus throat infection and Colburn rode all the way from Maine without mishap is either evidence of genetic constitution or doubt that it happened at all, given the travel conditions of the day. I can't say which. It isn't clear that the meeting would have made any difference, but it sure could have, given the influence of Washington. After all, he wrote the contract to Colburn in the first place.

But it was not to be. Throughout the remainder of his life, Colburn's claim failed. The family made several attempts over subsequent years, the last in 1857, to convince Congress to act in their favor, but all failed. Long after his death, the case of Reuben Colburn simply faded into history.

Chapter 12

THE TWILIGHT

D uring the last decades of his life, Reuben Colburn concerned himself with home, hearth and family. His holdings were still extensive, even by the standards of the time, although as in Jefferson's case, ready cash was scarce, especially from 1807 on, when the furniture had to be carried off to clear debts. The home was in function a working farm with hay fields, cows, hogs, chickens and the trappings of the rural agrarian life espoused by Jefferson. It was like a more modest version of Monticello without its questionable labor force, and it included a working office, in this case for shipbuilding.

Captain Oliver Colburn died young in September 1788 of mysterious causes thought to be a contagion picked up in the West Indies on a trading voyage. His grave site is unknown, but sources believe it to be behind the Congregational church near the mansion. Reuben interred him and comforted his wife, Margaret, who must have been crestfallen over his untimely death at forty-four. She moved back to Hallowell after his death, leaving the house and land to her children, John and his wife, Olive,[1] in particular. Younger brother Benjamin, the lieutenant in the militia, died in 1813 from complications of influenza, which struck hard in Pittston that year. Once again, the family returned to the graveyard to bury a younger man. In 1792, word came to Pittston that their beloved Governor Hancock had passed on in Boston. Colburn and Elizabeth made the long trip to Quincy to be in attendance at this national memorial to a great fellow Patriot. Major Colburn was an old man witnessing the limitations of mortality.

In 1795, two more trips were made to the cemetery behind the church. In that year, two of Reuben's sons perished. Ebenezer was lost at sea at sixteen, and his namesake, Reuben Jr., died at just twenty-five from unknown causes. Only David was left to carry on the business. Word came in 1811 from Orono by way of his nephew, William, that his older brother Jeremiah Jr., the fierce Patriot four years his senior, was also gone. Reuben saw his parents go, all of his brothers and two of his sons. It must have been a difficult load to bear. He was to be the enduring rock the community depended on right up to the end of his illustrious stay.

On a crisp fall afternoon, September 16, 1818, Reuben Colburn retired early to his bed opposite the room he had given to Benedict Arnold six days shy of forty-three years earlier. Reuben died. He was seventy-eight. Elizabeth and David erected a towering stone pillar in his memory, a metaphor for the man now laid to rest beneath it. This time it was in a new graveyard, Riverside, right down the road from the mansion. Elizabeth joined her husband in August 1821, one year after her husband's dream of Maine statehood was finally realized. David joined them five years later. His wife, Hannah Averill Colburn, remained in the family home until her death in 1870. "A light burned in her room for eight years," wrote Bertha A. Colburn, her granddaughter.[2] Following a hip injury in 1862, while reaching for tea at the fireplace in the dining room, she was confined to a "wheeled chair" from there on. Colburn House would always be a "house of widows."

In the home before his premature death, David started a long line of improvements to his father's original structure. In Reuben's time, the house lacked the ell addition now present, and life was at its most basic. All cooking was done in the fireplace of the keeping room, and of course, there was no indoor plumbing until the 1950s, and there still isn't in the main house. The single front door was offset to line up with the middle window on the second floor, as was the practice when Reuben built it in 1765. The family, neighbors and Indians who came and went would gather by the fireplace for warmth and camaraderie.

In keeping with the Federal period style, David installed a new, wider front door with sidelights and a new stairwell with a rounded wall and rebuilt the fireplace column. Aside from other superficial changes, that is the way the home is now. In 1953, when the home passed from the family for the last time, the new owners, the Paul Plumer family, found the house in disrepair after years of having no one living in it year round since Bertha's death in 1941. In the attic, Mrs. Plumer found a tin box of papers dated 1840, containing property of Captain David Lawrence, a sea captain who was married to Elizabeth, Gustavus Colburn's older sister. Lawrence died "at sea" in 1850, leaving his widow in grief and lost. She tended Concord grapevines "southwest of the flower garden" as therapy for her loss after just eight years of marriage.[3] A twenty-eight-star flag was found belonging to an "R.H. Colburn," probably Richard, Bertha's younger brother, or maybe Captain Reuben Colburn Jr., Major Colburn's grandson, one of the last to attempt to collect the claim money. A collection of swords, one of which was the major's, was also found. The flag is in the possession of the Lincoln County Historical Society in Wiscasset.[4] The swords have been lost. The valuable historic family documents, whatever this might have encompassed, were once "in the old house in the desk drawer in the west chamber," Bertha wrote, "the room Arnold occupied in his sojourn in Gardinerston, or town, or Pittston."[5] Not knowing the whereabouts or having these documents is a great tragedy. The Plumers, for all their great diligence with the flag, have to get the credit for bungling the family records if, in fact, they were left where Bertha claimed just before her death in 1941. Her memoir, written for her niece Helen Pomeroy, was left to the Arnold Society, and one would think had she had the papers in her possession she would have done the same with those, but there is nothing. Her parents, Richard and Idell, may have taken them. Idell died in Exeter, California, in 1904. Richard's demise is unknown. Helen died in the 1970s and is buried in Riverside Cemetery in Pittston with her Aunt Bertha.

The major's wine closet, where the punchbowl[6] from which Arnold and company "regaled themselves" was located, is built into the corner of the room, with "graceful curves." Although its authenticity is disputed, it is from "his time." Behind it is the hand-split lathe Reuben installed in 1765, and in the parlor, his wainscot-paneled walls remain the same. The home and legacy of Major Reuben Colburn remain, like the man, a testament to our time.

EPILOGUE

I t would be difficult to find two partners in history more ridiculed, scorned
and socially exiled than Benedict Arnold and Aaron Burr, but these are
the two characters my grandfather became involved with. Men make history
without the knowledge of how it will turn out. Tenuous was Colburn's
connection to the younger Burr, but he was present during the events
of that fall of 1775, as was Arnold. The story did not come out well for
either of them, and Reuben Colburn seems to have been muddied by their
presence in his life, even though he had nothing to do with either the actions
or character flaws that ultimately did this duo in, nor did he present any
evidence of sharing these traits. Likewise, neither did his close relationships
with the revered Washington and Hancock redeem him. All were on the way
up at that point and did their best to see that their effort produced a country
of their own design. It would seem they did.

Arnold died in disgrace in London in 1801, as Burr became vice president
under Thomas Jefferson, who had been driven from his Virginia farm by the
renegade Arnold serving in the British army. Burr was later tried for treason
while still in this office, and he killed his rival Hamilton in 1804, without
immediate consequence. It is hard to believe. The quest for glory demanded
great sacrifice and a strong personal constitution if one were to succeed. In
the end, critics will comb the record to see if the effort passed muster, but
the tendency to demonize was evident. In life, we have to take the good
with the bad, not just one or the other, and neither could be "invented."
History condemned the more infamous of this trio, but it is my hope that

this account will vindicate Reuben Colburn from the sullied stars he shared the stage with, for in that month of October 1775, they were our brightest beacons of freedom in the wilderness.

POSTSCRIPT

In the summer of 2000, I began researching the Colburn story after hearing a relative lament on the sorry condition of the Reuben Colburn House in Pittston, Maine. Though owned by the state since 1971, it had few funds for upkeep, and the house was sinking and rotting out from under the caretakers. I recalled the historical sign posted on Route 27 marking the turn on Arnold Road to the historic home and knew I was related to the former owner, but my family never talked about it much, and no one really knew much about him or his story. They just had the same last name. I thought the story would make a good movie; I still do, and to date no one has made it. I made a trip back to the house and talked with the caretaker, the then president of the Arnold Expedition Historical Society that leased the house from the state. It was a no-cost lease, a Department of Conservation historic site specialist explained.

The question I had was, did they all go on the expedition? The caretaker didn't know. "We think only the brothers went," he said. I was determined to find out, and the result is this book. Interest in the house and story built, and the state secured some funds to begin renovating the sinking house. This took place in stages over the last decade. I decided to pursue National Landmark status for the home but quickly ran into opposition from the National Park Service and the Maine Historic Preservation Commission based on what specialists deem "historic fabric issues." There had been many alterations since 1775, and these prevented such a high level of designation. I met fierce opposition. Eventually, I lowered my application to a separate listing on the National Register of Historic Places. Previously, it had been included, although not named, in the Arnold Historic District on that federal register. I wrote the fifty-page nomination form and submitted it. After much deliberation, the Colburn House State Historic Site became official in the federal register in 2004.

Today, renovations continue on the barn and carriage house, although the main house is restored back to the way it largely was in Reuben's day. The David Colburn entryway and rounded staircase was preserved. There are no resident caretakers, and reenactors don period clothing for special events open to the public. Artifacts from the expedition found along the route are displayed, and the museum library is still located inside the side door, where books can be purchased for those wanting to learn more.

THE GENEALOGY OF THE COLBURN FAMILY OF PITTSTON, MAINE

This genealogical analysis concerns the ancestors of Pittston, Maine, only. The ancestral Colburn family originates in the county of North Riding in Yorkshire, England, where they formed from the Anglo-Saxons between the eleventh and twelfth centuries. The family held land in many areas and were prominent in stature in English history. The name had many variations but is believed to mean "cold stream," a "burn" being such a body of water in Scotland, whereas the family name was found on the banks of a stream called Colburn Beck north of the city of York, a tributary of the River Swale. That's close enough to Scotland to fit this definition. An ancient Roman road was just a stone's throw away.

While the descendants of Edward who now bear the name of Coburn and Colburn are numerous and can be found in every state of the Union, those concerned with the founding of Maine are the focus here and were my immediate family. Abner Coburn, descended from the Dracut Coburns, a distant future cousin of Reuben, was an early settler of Skowhegan who became the governor of Maine in the 1800s. A complete genealogical chart is available on request.

Colburn House, 1901, by
Justin H. Smith. *Courtesy of
The Maine Historic Preservation
Commission.*

Colburn House front. *Author's collection.*

Above: Carriage house at Colburn House. *Author's collection.*

Below: Colburn meadow, site of Colburn's shipyard. *Author's collection.*

Grave of Major Colburn and Elizabeth. *Author's collection.*

Above, left: DAR plaque at Colburn House. *Author's collection.*

Above, right: William Colburn. *Author's collection.*

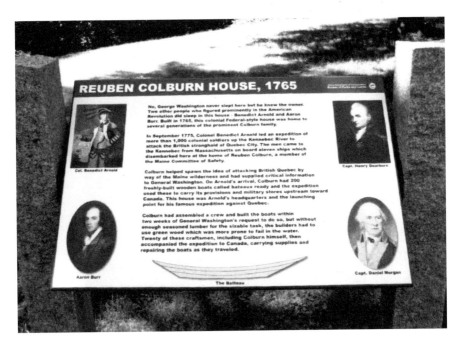

Interpretive Display at Colburn House. *Author's collection.*

NOTES

ACKNOWLEDGEMENTS

1. Roberts, *Trending into Maine*, 302–3. "Not one of the soldiers of Arnold's expedition made mention of the banquet; and there isn't even a chance one of them saw anything resembling a banquet; but Local Tradition saw it all, with its genius for seeing the wrong thing saw it all." Maybe the Dearborn, Senter and Meigs banquet accounts don't count in the Kennebunkport traditional eye?
2. Roberts, *March to Quebec*, 40, n. 23. "All the men from Arundel, Province of Maine, were in Goodrich's Company."
3. Roberts, "Foundation of a Maine Family," Chap. 5 in *Trending into Maine*, 103.
4. *Massachusetts Soldiers and Sailors*, 743. "Colburn, Oliver, Gardnerstown. Captain of a company of minutemen Col. Arnold's Regt; engaged July 25th 1775; engaged 20 days." The engagement dates and the actual service date are unclear or unrelated, but the mention of Arnold's company is clear, unlike in the case of Mr. Nason, the celebrated relative of our illustrious author. Reuben's service is well documented elsewhere in this text.
5. Ibid., vol. 11, 288. "Nason, Edward, Arundel. Private, Capt. Jesse Dorman's co., Col. James Scammon's (30th) Regt.; muster roll dated Aug. 1, 1775; enlisted May 8, 1775; service 3 mos.; also, company return

[probably October 1775] (this would place him on the retreat with Enos not attacking Quebec), including abstract of pay to last of July 1775." As the Arnold expedition didn't even leave until September 15, arriving at Colburn's on the twentieth, Mr. Nason's presence is at best foggy but a possibility if the assertion is true. Compare to the entry for Captain Oliver Colburn in the previous note.

CHAPTER 1

1. Merrill, *Colburn Family*, 1.
2. Ibid. See also Kingsbury and Deyo, *Illustrated History of Kennebec County*, 720.

CHAPTER 2

1. Hanson, *History of Gardiner.*
2. Ibid.
3. "Genealogical Records: Maine and N.H. settlers, 1600–1900s," *Historical and Genealogical Recorder* 6, no. 1 (1889): 286.
4. Hanson, "Incorporation," Chap. 4 in *History of Gardiner*.
5. Ibid.
6. Ibid.
7. *Lincoln County Records*, vol. 10, 39.
8. Ibid., 287.
9. U.S. Census, *1790 Winthrop, Me.*
10. "Genealogical Records," 182.
11. Ibid., 264.
12. Hanson, "Incorporation," Chap. 4 in *History of Gardiner*.

CHAPTER 3

1. Martin, *Benedict Arnold*, 18.
2. Ibid., 15.
3. Ibid.
4. Wilson, *Benedict Arnold*.
5. Ibid., 7.

6. Martin, "A Person to Be Reckoned with in New Haven," Chap. 2 in *Benedict Arnold*, 34.

7. Ibid., 42.

8. Ibid., 43.

9. "Committees of Safety," Microsoft Encarta Online Encyclopedia 2002. encarta.msn.com.

10. Hanson, "Incorporation," Chap. 4 in *History of Gardiner*.

11. "The Quebec Act, 1774." www.solon.org/Constitutions/Canada/ English/PreConfederation/qa_1774.html.

Chapter 4

1. *Thomas Jefferson Papers*, Library of Congress, Series 1. General Correspondence; John Adams to Thomas Jefferson, August 24, 1815, 375.

2. Smith, *Arnold's March*, 299, n. 10, n. 16.

3. Ibid., notes to pages 74–83; 299, 300, n. 16; 298–99, n. 10.

4. Roberts, *Trending into Maine*, 297.

5. Hanson, "Indian History," Chap. 1 in *History of Gardiner*.

6. Smith, *Our Struggle*, 501.

7. Randall, *Benedict Arnold*, 136. From Middlekauf, *Glorious Cause*, 300–1.

8. National Park Service, *Head Quarters, Cambridge: Washington's Occupancy of the Longfellow House*. www.nps.gov/long, lnhstest.brinkster.net/Level2/house/ HouseEssay/WashingtonsHQ.html.

9. Ibid.

10. Hanson, *History of Gardiner*.

11. Fitzpatrick, *Writings of George Washington*, vol. 3, n. 99, "Letter to Schuyler."

12. Massachusetts Archives, *Legislative Records of the Council*, xxxiii, 118, ccvi, 246, House Journal, 77.

13. Fitzpatrick, *Writings of George Washington*, "Letter to Schuyler."

14. Ibid., "Reuben Colburn to George Washington, August 20, 1775," Revolutionary War Accounts, Vouchers, and Receipted Accounts 2.

15. Ibid., 35.

16. Washington, *George Washington Papers*, Library of Congress, Letter, "BA to Reuben Colburn," 1:409:10. Originals are in the National Archives and Records Administration, "Claim of Reuben Colburn," HR 22A-G20.1

17. Ibid., ser. 3b, Varick Transcripts, "George Washington to Nathaniel Tracy, September 2, 1775."

18. Ibid., "Orders to Reuben Colburn, 3 September 1775," 111, 471.
19. Natanis.
20. Ibid., ser. 4, "General Correspondence," 323, 324. See also original in NARA file, n. 14.
21. Bird, *Attack on Quebec*, 78.
22. Washington, *George Washington Papers*, "General Orders, Sept. 5, 1775."
23. Hanson, Chap. 1 in *History of Gardiner.*
24. Randall, *Benedict Arnold*, 162.
25. Desjardin, *Through a Howling Wilderness*, 26.
26. Smith, *Arnold's March*, 79.
27. Ibid.
28. Ibid.
29. Hanson, *History of Gardiner*, 18, 19, 82.
30. History has been weak in telling this aspect of the story. The National Park Service firmly held that the Continental army only stayed at Fort Western and Colburn was "just a prominent contractor," not a big player in history on the national stage. Justin Smith of Dartmouth called Colburn "the fulcrum of the operation."
31. American Archives, 4th Series, 3:1083–84, "Samuel Goodwin to George Washington, Pownalborough, Oct. 17, 1775."
32. Ibid.; Smith, *Arnold's March*, 261. Goodwin's letters to the Reverend Jacob Bailey prove that he was a royalist at heart. But, as he was probably a "trimmer," he desired very likely to stand well with both sides.
33. Randall, *Benedict Arnold*, 152. Randall claims the maps were deliberately altered, but there is no evidence of this. They simply lacked the detail needed to avoid natural pitfalls.
34. This depends on how one measures and from where. Driving today up Route 201, it's 236 miles from Pittston to Quebec City, so the wilderness route is not far off from the 180-mile estimate from the maps provided by Colburn, Goodwin and Montresor.
35. Smith, *Arnold's March*, 261, n. 17. Explains this history.
36. John Montrésor, military engineer; b. April 22, 1736, at Gibraltar, son of James Gabriel Montresor and Mary Haswell; m. March 1, 1764, Frances Tucker, in New York City, and they had six surviving children; d. June 26, 1799, in Maidstone prison, England. www.biographi.ca/EN/ShowBio.asp?BioId=36197.
37. Merrill, *Colburn Family*. Hancock was the largest landowner in Pittston, and Colburn milled his lumber for many years. Colburn also cared for a wayward nephew of Hancock's.

38. Risch, "The Continental Army," Chap. 1 in *Supplying Washington's Army*, 20.

39. Susannah Grier and seventeen-year-old Jemima Warner.

40. Hanson, Chap. 1 in *History of Gardiner.*

41. Smith, *Arnold's March*, 82–83.

42. National Historic Landmark failed nomination in 2002. Some (i.e., historians at the National Park Service) have denied that the place where the expedition actually started was Colburn's shipyard and home.

43. Roberts, *March to Quebec*, "Thayer Journal," 248–49

44. Ibid., "Pierce."

45. Ibid., "Stocking," 546.

46. Ibid., "Henry," 302.

47. Ibid., "Senter," 198–99.

48. In Roberts, *March to Quebec*. Arnold's journal doesn't start until Fort Western.

49. Roberts, *March to Quebec*, "Oswald," 41.

50. Ibid., "Meigs," 174. Return Jonathan Meigs was born in Middletown, Connecticut, on December 17, 1734. He marched with a company of light infantry to the vicinity of Boston immediately after the Battle of Lexington and Concord and was assigned to duty under Colonel Benedict Arnold with the rank of major.

51. Roberts, *March to Quebec*, "Melvin," 436.

52. Roberts, "Road to the Past," Chap. 14 in *Trending into Maine*, 300.

53. Ibid., 301.

54. Colburn's. The journalists called him all sorts of permutations of the family name.

55. In his estimation.

56. Roberts, *March to Quebec*, "Squier," 629.

57. Washington, *George Washington Papers*, ser. 4, "Arnold Journal," 105.

58. Smith, *Our Struggle*, 524–25. This scene, as Smith said himself, is "inferential."

59. Smith, *Arnold's March*, 78.

60. Ibid., 296–97.

61. Roberts, *March to Quebec*, "Arnold's Account Sheets of the Quebec Expedition," 717–24.

62. Fitzpatrick, *Writings of George Washington*, n. 5. Aaron Burr served as a volunteer on the Canadian expedition of 1775, was lieutenant colonel of Malcolm's Additional Continental regiment in January 1777, resigned in March 1779, was vice president of the United States from 1801 to 1805 and died in 1836.

63. Merrill, *Colburn Family.*

Chapter 5

1. Ibid., "Address to the Citizens of Canada."
2. Huston, *Logistics of Arnold's March to Quebec*.
3. Roberts, *March to Quebec*, "Col. Arnold's Letters," 69.
4. National Archives, *Reuben Colburn*.
5. Roberts, *March to Quebec*, "Senter," 199. As Roberts noted, the Howards are the ancestors of the Gannetts of Portland, newspaper owners and restorers of the fort at Augusta. They have since sold the Maine papers to the *Seattle Times*.
6. Lomask, *Aaron Burr*, 38–39.
7. Roberts, *March to Quebec*, "Thayer," 249.
8. Ibid., "Haskell," 474.
9. Thomas Agry (1722/23–1783) was one of the first shipbuilders to settle on the Kennebec River above Bath. Agry's Point is located on the Kennebec about a half mile below the Colburn House.
10. Samuel Oakman (1745–1822) was a prosperous ship captain, shipbuilder and ship owner. He married Thomas Agry's daughter, Hannah, about 1772. The Oakman property was located south of Reuben Colburn's.
11. Colburn, *Memories of My Childhood*, 13.
12. Roberts, *Trending into Maine*, 304.
13. Parton, "His Relations with Women," Chap. 34 in *Life and Times of Aaron Burr*, 637–59.
14. Coolidge, *Colonial Entrepreneur*, 194–95. Kenneth Roberts denies this meal ever took place, but this author feels it is because his ancestors (i.e., Steven [Edward] Nason) wouldn't have been invited due to his low status in the expedition.
15. Roberts, *March to Quebec*, "Dearborn," 132.
16. Ibid., "Meigs," 175.
17. Smith, *Arnold's March*, 293–94. These are taken from the Reuben Colburn Papers Archives of Congress, RG 233, HR 22A-G20.1.
18. Roberts, *March to Quebec*, "Henry," 302–3.
19. Lomask, *Aaron Burr*, 38–39.
20. Roberts, *March to Quebec*, "Col. Arnold's Letters," 69. Date of letter and journal entry do not match: 29 and 28, respectively.
21. National Archives, *Reuben Colburn Papers*. See receipt from Samuel Berry for this birch canoe. Also see "Arnold's Journal," September 29, 1775, 40
22. Roberts, *March to Quebec*, "Senter," 200.

23. See Coburn, *Descendants of Edward Colburn*. Indians came and went from Colburn's house freely. His ancestors, the family of Edward Colburn, made peace with the Wamesits after they burned down the Colburn homes in Dracut, Massachusetts, in the late 1600s. Roberts also adopts this Colburn philosophy when it came to Abenakis.

24. www.nativeweb.org/pages/legal/amherst/34_40_305_fn.jpeg.

25. Maine Historical Society, Portland, Maine. Doc. 1368, "William Drew Letter Jan. 30, 1868."

26. Huston, *Logistics of Arnold's March to Quebec*, 4.

27. Private James McCormack. He committed a murder in the night at Fort Western. See Roberts, *March to Quebec*, "Thayer."

28. Sabatis and another.

29. Huston, *Logistics of Arnold's March to Quebec*, 4.

30. Around Ticonic Falls.

31. Roberts, *March to Quebec*, "Senter," 200–1.

32. Huston, *Logistics of Arnold's March to Quebec*, 4. This is true.

33. Ibid.

34. Ibid., 5.

35. Ibid., "Arnold," 46.

36. Colburn.

37. Roberts, *March to Quebec*, "Thayer," 250.

38. Ibid., "Morison," 511–12.

39. Randall claims Arnold ordered them "lap-straked," when there is nothing in his records indicating this stipulation.

40. Randall, *Benedict Arnold*, 162.

41. Frank S. Getchell brought this to my attention after I published a letter to the editor in the *Waterville Morning Sentinel* on March 23, 2004, about my film and book. It appears John Getchell was the guide with Henry, according to this research and the lack of genealogical evidence of a Jeremiah in that generation.

42. Randall, *Benedict Arnold*, "Henry," 320–21.

43. Roberts, *March to Quebec*, "Thayer," 250.

44. Ibid.

45. Ibid., "Senter," 203.

46. Ibid.

47. Ibid., "Arnold," 46–47.

48. Ibid.

49. Having fished the river where it enters the Kennebec, this author can attest that it is not navigable except by kayak or whitewater raft.

50. Roberts, *March to Quebec*, "Arnold," 49.

51. Ibid., "Morison," 520.

52. Ibid., 521.

53. Done in 1903, Justin Smith's work *Arnold's March from Cambridge to Quebec* looks at all the details of the march. Smith, of Dartmouth College, traveled the route himself and knew the relatives of the Colburn family living in Reuben's house at the turn of the twentieth century. I have no intention of repeating what he did but use it as a good reference point. Furthermore, few readers in bookstores today will find it on the shelf or would know of it in the first place. Like all of Smith's work, it is top notch. A reprint of the Smith book is available for sale at the Arnold Expedition Historical Society, located at Colburn House in Pittston, and at its website, www.aehs.com. Note: Smith is fiercely critical of the Codman book that preceded his work while it was still in progress. I have read it and agree, as do most historians, that Smith is right. This work is meant to be the most current thesis on the subject available and written by a modern member of the family.

54. Roberts, *March to Quebec*, "Senter," 205.

55. Ibid., "Arnold," 50.

56. Ibid., "Senter," 206.

57. Ibid., "Morison," 522.

58. Smith, *Arnold's March*, 304. "Cash paid Natannes the Indian for guiding us on our journey to Quebec 0:6:0 (Shillings)."

59. Bird, *Attack on Quebec*, 74–75. Bird misreads Natanis's role, claiming he "had not told them about the Mohawks at Sartigan, only the seven British soldiers." This was another unnamed Indian they met, possibly a Mohawk himself. Moreover, Reuben Colburn paid Natanis to guide Dennis Getchell and Samuel Berry on the initial scouting trip.

60. Randall, *Benedict Arnold*, 164, has Getchell and Berry meeting with Natanis on the Dead River. He guided Getchell and Berry and was not the one he met with who misinformed them of the conditions at Sartigan. Desjardin falls for the same thing in *Through a Howling Wilderness*, 31. It is unwise to trust the account of Henry.

61. Wilson and Fiske, *Appleton's Cyclopedia*. Christopher Greene was born in Warwick, Rhode Island, on May 12, 1737. He served in the Rhode Island legislature in 1772–74 and was chosen as a lieutenant in the Kentish Guards in 1774. In May 1775, he was appointed by the legislature a major in the army of observation, given command of a company, marched to Cambridge and subsequently was placed by Washington in command of

the first battalion under Arnold. Early in 1781, while in command on the Croton River, Greene's headquarters were surrounded by a party of Loyalists, by whom he was killed. He died in Westchester County, New York, on May 13, 1781.

62. Huston, *Logistics of Arnold's March to Quebec*, 6.

63. Major Timothy Bigelow of Worchester, Massachusetts, was a former blacksmith and a staunch Patriot who arrived in Cambridge in command of a company of minutemen in May 1775. He was given a commission in Ward's company, where he found himself in this current predicament. Mount Bigelow is named for him. Legend has it that he took the time and energy to climb the mountain in order to get a view of the way to Quebec, but this is doubtful, given his predicament and assignments at the time.

64. Roberts, *March to Quebec*, "Arnold's letters," 75.

65. Ibid., "Thayer," 254.

66. Ibid. Cartridges, paper packets of gunpowder.

67. Roberts, "Arnold's letters," 75.

68. Smith, *Arnold's March*, 154.

69. Ibid., 145.

70. Roberts, *March to Quebec*, "Arnold's letters," 75.

71. Ibid., "Thayer," 255.

72. Ibid.

73. Ibid., "Topham," 258.

74. Ibid., 256.

75. Smith, *Arnold's March*, 162.

76. Wilson and Fiske, *Appleton's Cyclopedia*, "Thayer." Simeon Thayer, born in Mendon, Massachusetts, on April 30, 1737, moved to Rhode Island as a youth and served in the French and Indian War in 1756 with the Rhode Island troops and with Major Robert Roger's Rangers. In 1757, he was taken prisoner at Fort William Henry. In May 1775, he was appointed captain by the Rhode Island assembly and assigned to the Arnold expedition.

77. Roberts, *March to Quebec*, "Thayer," 256.

78. Wilson and Fiske, *Appleton's Cyclopedia*, "Enos." Colonel Roger Enos was born in Simsbury, Connecticut, in 1729. He was in the colonial service during the French and Indian War in 1759 and became ensign in March 1760, lieutenant in September 1760, adjutant of his regiment and captain lieutenant in 1761, first lieutenant in 1762 and captain in Israel Putnam's regiment in 1764. He faced desertion charges that he "returned with his command, to avoid starvation, on October 25 of that

year, and on Dec. 1, 1775 was tried at a court martial for 'quitting without leave,' and 'honorably acquitted'" for his decision on the Dead River. He died in Colchester, Vermont, on October 6, 1808. Enos was the oldest commander on the expedition.

79. Roberts, *March to Quebec*, "Thayer," 257.

80. Ibid., "Squier," 624. Squier lived to be ninety-four.

81. Ibid., 623.

82. Ibid., 625.

83. Ibid., "Henry," 320.

84. See n. 134. John Getchell is believed to be the guide here, not Jeremiah.

85. Dennis, who led the recon mission with Berry, isn't recorded as being on the actual expedition.

86. Roberts, *March to Quebec*, "Meigs," 180. "Meigs to Nehemiah Getchell and Samuel Berry for guiding duties; 44 and 45 dollars respectively." The Getchells—Jeremiah? (John), Nehemiah and Dennis of Vassalborough— all participated in the expedition in a prominent way at the request of Reuben Colburn.

87. Smith, *Arnold's March*, 293–97, n. 6; Huston, *Logistics of Arnold's March to Quebec*, 3. Final action on Colburn's claim did not come until March 1824, when Congress refused to approve payment largely on the ground that the lapse of so much time, and the loss of public records, made the justice of the claim doubtful. U.S. government, *Annals of Congress*, March 12, 1824, 338, and March 15, 1824, 342–43. Family members carried on the fight in Congress until 1856.

88. Smith, *Arnold's March*, 317, note 28.

CHAPTER 6

1. Ibid., 164.

2. Roberts, *March to Quebec*, "Arnold," 56.

3. Ibid.

4. Ibid., 56–57.

5. Ibid.

6. Ibid., 58, n. 38.

7. Ibid.

8. Ibid., "Arnold," 59.

9. Smith, *Arnold's March*, 415, n. 8.

10. Ibid., 200.

11. Ibid.
12. Ibid.
13. Roberts, *March to Quebec*, "Arnold," 59.
14. Ibid., "Montresor," 23. Roberts mentions this is because Montresor passed through at night.
15. Ibid.
16. Ibid., "Colonel Arnold's Letters," 79.
17. Ibid.
18. Ogden, *Journal of Mathias Ogden*, 4.
19. Ibid.
20. Ibid.
21. Ibid.
22. Ibid.
23. Ibid.
24. Ibid, 5.
25. Ibid.
26. Ibid.
27. Roberts, *March to Quebec*, "Dearborn," 138.
28. This may be the Ayres who was a partner with Jeremiah Colburn Jr. in his Orono, Maine operation. That Colburn was later captured by the British at the Camden arsenal.
29. Roberts, *March to Quebec*, "Melvin," 439.
30. Ibid.
31. Ibid., "Dearborn," 139.
32. Ibid.
33. Ogden, *Journal of Mathias Ogden*, 6.
34. Ibid.
35. Ibid.
36. Ibid.
37. Ibid., 7.
38. Roberts, *March to Quebec*, "Senter."
39. Ibid., "Stocking," 556.
40. Randall, *Benedict Arnold*, 185. Randall has Jacataqua and two Indians rescuing Greene's company. It was Natanis, and there is no mention of Burr, who, if the legendary Jacataqua character is real, would have been with him.
41. Roberts, *March to Quebec*, "Fobes."
42. Ibid., "Pierce," 664.
43. Ibid., 667.

44. Ibid., 668.
45. Ibid., "Arnold," 60.
46. Ibid., 80.
47. Ibid., "Pierce," 670.
48. Ibid., "Senter," 219.
49. Ibid.
50. Ibid., "Thayer," 261.
51. Ibid., 671.

CHAPTER 7

1. Ogden, *Journal of Mathias Ogden*, 7.
2. Ibid.
3. Roberts, *March to Quebec*, "Henry," 344–45.
4. Ibid.
5. Randall, *Benedict Arnold*, 196. Randall makes no mention of Colburn in recounting this story and claims that help in guiding the expedition was refused by Washington. It wasn't. Colburn hired Natanis as a guide.
6. Davis, *Memoirs of Aaron Burr*, 67.
7. Ibid., 68.
8. Ibid., 8.
9. Ibid., 10.
10. Ibid.
11. Ibid.
12. Roberts, *March to Quebec*, "Fobes," 586.
13. Ibid.
14. Ogden, *Journal of Mathias Ogden*, 10
15. Ibid.
16. Ibid., 12.
17. Huston, *Logistics of Arnold's March to Quebec*, 3.
18. Ogden, *Journal of Mathias Ogden*, 13.
19. Ibid.
20. Ibid.
21. Ibid., 14.

CHAPTER 8

1. Ibid.
2. In Ogden, *Journal of Mathias Ogden.*
3. Ibid.
4. Ibid.
5. Ibid.
6. Roberts, *March to Quebec*, "Haskell," 482.
7. Ibid., 483, n. 4.
8. Ibid.
9. Ibid., 273.
10. Ibid., "Meigs," 189.
11. Ibid.
12. Washington, *George Washington Papers*, "David Wooster to Philip J. Schuyler, January 5, 1775."
13. Ibid., 191.
14. Hanson, "Indian History," Chap. 1 in *History of Gardiner.*
15. Roberts, *March to Quebec*, "Fobes," 600–1.
16. Ibid., 608–9.
17. Ibid., 613.
18. Huston, *Logistics of Arnold's March to Quebec*, 12.
19. Ibid.
20. McCullough, "The Road to Philadelphia," Chap. 1 in *John Adams*, 28.
21. *Danvers Courier*, July 17, 1845.

CHAPTER 9

1. *Massachusetts Soldiers and Sailors of the Revolutionary War.*
2. Coburn, "Jeremiah Colburn Jr.," in *Genealogy of the Descendants of Edward Colburn*, 87–88.
3. Sprague, *Journal of Maine History*, 202.

CHAPTER 10

1. Parker, *History of Farmington*, 23, 52.
2. Ibid.
3. Ibid.

4. Ibid.

5. Ibid.

6. Ibid.

7. Hanson, *History of Gardiner*, 150

8. Merrill, *Colburn Family.*

9. Ibid., 16.

10. Baker, *Maritime History of Bath*, 94.

11. Fairburn, *Merchant Sail*, 3321–22.

12. Rowe, *Maritime History of Maine*, 56.

13. Ibid.

14. Hutchins, *American Maritime Industries*, 180.

15. Merrill, *Colburn Family*, 4.

16. Fairburn, *Merchant Sail*, 321.

CHAPTER 11

1. Hanson, "Sketch of Pittston from the Separation," Chap. 5 in *History of Gardiner*.

2. Ian Finseth, "Political Battles, Secretary of the Treasury," Chap. 3 in *Rise and Fall of Alexander Hamilton*.

3. American Memory, Library of Congress, *A Century of Lawmaking for a New Nation: U.S. Congressional Documents and Debates, 1774–1875* 36th Congress, May, 4, 1860 H.R. 686.

4. Schamel, et al., *Guide to the Records of the United States House of Representatives.*

5. Huston, *Logistics of Arnold's March to Quebec*, 10.

6. Washington, *George Washington Papers*, 33.

7. Roberts, *March to Quebec*, 68.

8. Smith, *Arnold's March*, 293–94. These are taken from the Reuben Colburn Papers Archives of Congress RG 233, HR 22A-G20.1

9. Ibid.

10. Ibid., 299–300.

11. Daughters of the American Revolution.

12. Ibid.

13. Ibid.

14. Archives of Congress, "The Claim of Reuben Colburn," RG233, Records of the U.S. House of Representatives, Committee on Revolutionary Claims, HR22A-G20.1.

15. Hanson, "Settlement and Incorporation," in *History of Gardiner*, 79.

16. Ibid., "Berry," 1795.
17. American Memory at the Library of Congress, "U.S. Congressional Documents and Debates, 1774–1873," Annals of Congress House of Representatives, 4th Congress, 1st Session, 269.
18. The Mount Vernon Ladies Association found no written record of this visit in Washington's journals or house records. Naturally, they were concerned with the health and demise of the president.
19. Coburn, *Descendants of Edward Colburn*, 89.

Chapter 12

1. Reuben's daughter. They married in 1807.
2. Colburn, *Memories of My Childhood*, 4.
3. Ibid., 1.
4. Maxwell, "House where Benedict Arnold Slept."
5. Colburn, *Memories of My Childhood*, 14.
6. Merrill, *Colburn Family*, 4.

BIBLIOGRAPHY

American Archives, 4ᵗʰ Series. Samuel Goodwin to George Washington, Pownalborough, MA. October 17, 1775.

Baker, William Avery. *A Maritime History of Bath Maine and the Kennebec River Region.* Vol. 1. Bath, ME, 1973.

Bell, William Gardner. *Commanding Generals and Chiefs of Staff 1775 to 1995.* "Henry Dearborn." Washington, D.C.: Center of Military History United States Army, 1995.

Bird, Harrison. *Attack on Quebec: The American Invasion of Canada 1775.* New York: Oxford University Press, 1968.

Coburn, Frederick W. "Forestry at the Maine Coburns Old Home in Massachusetts." *Lewiston Journal,* May 1936.

Coburn, Silas Roger, and George Augustus Gordon. *Genealogy of the Descendants of Edward Colburn.* Lowell, MA: W. Coburn, 1913.

Colburn, Bertha A. *Memories of My Childhood.* N.p.: AEHS, 2001.

Coolidge, Olivia E. *Colonial Entrepreneur: Dr. Sylvester Gardiner and the Settlement of Maine's Kennebec Valley.* Gardiner, ME: Tilbury House Publishers and Gardiner Library Association, 1999.

Davis, Matthew L. *Memoirs of Aaron Burr.* New York: Harper & Brothers, 1836.

Desjardin, Thomas A. *Through a Howling Wilderness: Benedict Arnold's March to Quebec 1775.* New York: St. Martin's Press, 2006.

Dunnack, Henry E. *The Maine Book.* Augusta, ME, 1920.

Fairburn, William Armstrong. *Merchant Sail.* Vol. 5. Glasgow, Scotland: University of Glasgow, 1897.

Finseth, Ian. "Political Battles, Secretary of the Treasury." Chap. 3 in *The Rise and Fall of Alexander Hamilton*. Charlottesville: University of Virginia, n.d.

Fitzpatrick, John C., ed. *The Writings of George Washington from the Original Manuscript Sources, 1745–1799*. N.p., n.d.

"Genealogical Records: Maine and N.H. Settlers, 1600–1900s." *Historical and Genealogical Recorder* 6, no. 1 (1889).

Hanson, J.W. *History of Gardiner, Pittston, and West Gardiner, 1602 to 1852*. Gardiner, ME: William Palmer, 1852.

Huguenots in America. *French Settlement in Maine*. N.p., n.d.

Huston, James A. *The Logistics of Arnold's March to Quebec*. American Military Institute. *Military Analysis of the Revolutionary War: An Anthology by the Editors of Military Affairs*. Millwood, NY: KTO Press, 1977.

Hutchins, John G.B. *The American Maritime Industries and Public Policy, 1789–1914: An Economic History*. Cambridge, MA: Harvard University Press, 1941.

Kingsbury, Henry D., and Simeon L. Deyo, eds. *Illustrated History of Kennebec County, Maine, 1662–1892*. New York: H.W. Blake and Company, 1892.

Lomask, Milton. *Aaron Burr: The Years From Princeton to Vice-President, 1756–1085*. New York: Farrar, Strauss, Giroux, 1979.

Martin, James Kirby. "A Childhood of Legends. Chap. 1 in *Benedict Arnold Revolutionary Hero: An American Warrior Reconsidered*. New York: New York University Press, 1997.

Massachusetts Soldiers and Sailors of the Revolutionary War. Vol. 3. Boston, 1896–1908.

Maxwell, Grace. "House Where Benedict Arnold Slept Being Restored." *Kennebec Journal*, 1956.

McCullough, David. "The Road to Philadelphia." Chap. 1 in *John Adams*. New York: Simon & Schuster, 2008.

Merrill, Virginia T. *Colburn Family of Pittston Maine. Maine State Library*. Maine Historical Society, Portland, ME. Doc. 1368, William Drew Letter Jan. 30, 1868.

Middlekauf, Robert. *The Glorious Cause: The American Revolution, 1763–1789*. N.p.: Oxford University Press, rev. exp. edition, 2007.

National Archives and Records Administration, Washington D.C. *The Reuben Colburn Papers*. The Center for Legislative Archives, Record Group 233, Records of the U.S. House of Representatives, Committee on Revolutionary Claims, Petitions and Memorials, Claim of Reuben Colburn, HR 22A-G20.1. 1796.

Ogden, Mathias. *Journal of Mathias Ogden, 1775, in Arnold's Campaign Against Quebec*. Original in the Possession of the Washington Association of New Jersey, Morristown, NJ. 1928.

Parker, Thomas, Judge of Probate. *History of Farmington 1846*. N.p.: J.S. Swift, 1875.

Parton, J. "His Relations with Women." Chap. 34 in *The Life and Times of Aaron Burr.* New York: Mason Brothers, 1858.

Randall, Willard Sterne. *Benedict Arnold: Patriot and Traitor.* New York: William Morrow & Co., July 1990.

Risch, Erna. "The Continental Army." Chap. 1 in *Supplying Washington's Army.* N.p., 1981.

Roberts, Kenneth Lewis. *Arundel.* N.p., 1930.

―――. *March to Quebec: The Journals of the Members of the Arnold Expedition.* N.p., 1932.

―――. *Trending into Maine.* Illustrations by N.C. Wyeth. Boston: Little, Brown and Co., 1938.

Rowe, William Hutchinson. *The Maritime History of Maine.* New York: W.W. Norton & Company, 1948.

Schamel, Charles E., Mary Rephlo, Rodney Ross, David Kepley, Robert W. Coren and James Gregory Bradsher. *Guide to the Records of the United States House of Representatives at the National Archives, 1789–1989.* Bicentennial Edition (Doct. No. 100-245). 6.6. Washington, D.C.: National Archives and Records Administration, 1989.

Smith, Justin H. *Arnold's March from Cambridge to Quebec: A Critical Study, Together with a Reprint of Arnold's Journal.* New York: G. Putnam's Sons, 1903.

―――. *Our Struggle for the Fourteenth Colony: Canada and the American Revolution.* 2 vols. New York: G.P. Putnam's Sons, 1907.

Sprague, John F. *Journal of Maine History.* Vol. 2. N.p., n.d.

United Church of Christ. *A Short Course in Congregationalism.* N.p., n.d.

U.S. Government. *Annals of Congress.* Senate, 18th Congress, 1st Session, Case of Reuben Colburn, March 12, 1824, and March 15, 1824.

Washington, George. *The George Washington Papers.* Library of Congress. Instructions to Arnold (drafted by Thomas Mifflin).

―――. *The George Washington Papers.* Library of Congress. Letter Washington to Nathaniel Tracy, 2 September 1775; see Washington to Gov. Jonathan Trumbull, September 2, 1775.

―――. *The George Washington Papers.* Library of Congress. Orders to Reuben Colburn, September 3, 1775.

Webster, Henry S. ed. *Vital Records of Pittston, Maine, to the Year 1892.* Gardiner, ME: Reporter-Journal Press, 1911.

Wilson, Barry K. *Benedict Arnold: A Traitor in Our Midst.* N.p.: McGill-Queens University Press, 2001.

Wilson, James Grant, and John Fiske, eds. *Appleton's Cyclopedia of American Biography.* 6 vols. New York: D. Appleton and Company, 1887–89.

INDEX

About the Author

M ark A. York is a journalist, biologist and novelist. He has worked as a carpenter, actor and fisheries biologist all over the West and Alaska and was a full-time reporter at the *Livingston Enterprise* in Livingston, Montana. He has written a blog that focuses on environmental issues since 2003 and wrote special projects in 2011 for the *Idaho Mountain Express* in Ketchum, Idaho, where he resides. He is a member of the Screen Actors Guild and the United Brotherhood of Carpenters and Joiners of America.